THE HANDBOOK
OF HOUSEHOLD
HINTS & TIPS

THE HANDBOOK OF
HOUSEHOLD
HINTS & TIPS

Maria Costantino

ISLAND BOOKS

This edition published in 2003 by

S.WEBB & Son (Distributors) LTD

Telford Place, Pentraeth Road,

Menai Bridge,

Isle of Anglesey,LL59 5RW

© 2003 D&S Books Ltd

D&S Books Ltd
Kerswell,
Parkham Ash, Bideford
Devon, England
EX39 5PR

e-mail us at:-
enquiries@dsbooks.fsnet.co.uk

This edition printed 2003

ISBN 1-85605-763-1

All rights reserved. This book is protected by copyright. No part of it may be reproduced, stored in a retrieval system, or transmitted in any form or by any means, without the prior permission in writing of the Publisher, nor be circulated in any form of binding or cover other than that in which it is published and without a similar condition including this condition being imposed on the subsequent Publisher

Creative Director: Sarah King
Editor: Clare Haworth-Maden
Project Editor: Judith Millidge
Photographer: Colin Bowling
Designer: Dave Jones

Typeset in Helvetica Neue

Printed in China

1 3 5 7 9 10 8 6 4 2

CONTENTS

Introduction 6

1 Spit and polish: cleaning your house 21
Order in the house 22
Cleaning and maintaining flooring. 23
Carpets and rugs 30
Walls and ceilings 40
Let there be light: cleaning windows,
    glass and mirrors 43
Curtains and blinds. 45
Soft furnishing and upholstery 48
Caring for furniture 51
Precious things 58
Atmospherics 61
Tips for the bedroom. 63
Keeping your bathroom sparkling 65
Caring for your kitchen 69

2 Kitchen and food tips 85
Stocking up: top tips for grocery shopping . . . 87
The store cupboard 91
The refrigerator 98
Freezers and ice-box compartments 100
Food-hygiene tips. 104
Oven temperatures. 106
Chef's tips. 106

3 Wardrobes and laundry 127
Care labels 128
Machine-washing preparations 132
Hand-washing tips 134
When to soak clothes 135
Whiter than white: bleaching 136
Tackling spots and stains. 137

An expert guide to stain removal. 142
Drying tips. 149
Ironing laundry. 151
Storing clothes. 155
Looking after shoes and boots 159
Caring for accessories. 161

4 Looking good from head to toe. 163
Know your skin type 165
A daily skincare routine 166
Special facial treatments 171
Full body treatments 174
The eyes have it! 176
Your crowning glory 178
Caring for your teeth 182
Hands and feet. 184
Finishing touches 187

5 Home maintenance 189
Home decorating: paint 192
Wallpaper 209
DIY tips. 217
Conserving energy 224

6 Green fingers 227
Caring for flowers. 228
Caring for houseplants 235
Container gardening 240
In the garden 244
Easy-going, easy-growing herbs. 249

Index 251
Credits and acknowledgements 255

INTRODUCTION

Whether your home is a mansion or a bedsit, a country cottage or city loft, a great deal of time, energy and expense has been invested in it. Running a home isn't just about keeping it clean, it's about feeling comfortable in it when you come home after a hard day at work. Successful home management consequently involves looking after the things that are important to you: the fabric of your home, your wardrobe and, most importantly, yourself.

Most people regard household chores as a bore; some think that if they ignore them, it won't matter; and many people just don't have a clue about household chores because they were always done for them, be it by their parents or older siblings. Looking after a home requires common sense, but there is also a great deal of knowledge and skill involved. One thing is perfectly true: unless you employ a professional housekeeper to look after your home – and even then there are limits to what people will do – you can't rely on the household fairies to come in while you're out at work or asleep and magic away your mess. Sooner or later, something will have to be done about the pile of washing up in the kitchen sink, the bundle of dirty laundry lurking in the bathroom or the growing glacier in your refrigerator.

Whether you've just left home and have moved into your own place, or you have to hide behind the sofa and pretend you're not at home when friends

drop by unexpectedly because your place looks like burglars have ransacked it, you'll need to sort out your home. And what's the point of spending your hard-earned salary on fabulous clothes and shoes if you don't know how to keep them – and yourself – looking like you've just stepped out of the pages of a glossy magazine?

In this book you'll find hundreds of useful and effective hints, tips and bright ideas to help you to deal with household chores, as well as many more to help you to shape up your home and free up your time to spend on other activities. Don't worry – you won't suddenly turn into a compulsive cleaner or become so obsessive that you can't sleep at night because one of your coat hangers is facing the wrong way! But you will find that you can make light work of necessary jobs, save a bit of time and money and, who knows, you may even find that you actually enjoy looking after, and taking a pride in, your home and possessions.

Getting organised

Whether you live alone, with your family or with a group of friends in a shared house, the key to running a home successfully is organisation. Organisation doesn't have to be carried out with military precision, although you may find that you need to develop a little more personal discipline. Imagine what would happen at work if your co-workers got stuck in traffic one day and you were left in charge. What would you do to hold the fort? What job would you start to do first? At work, most of us dream of running the place and, given the opportunity, we would rise to the challenge, give it our best shot and probably do quite well under the circumstances. If you can run a business in an emergency, then you should be able to run your home with your eyes shut.

The only right way of doing things is the way that is right for you, so make sure that your system for tackling household chores suits your lifestyle, your energy and your schedule. Be honest with yourself: are you useless in the mornings, but come alive in the evenings? Don't make yourself do things when your natural energy levels are low, but instead work out a timetable and schedule your tasks for high-energy periods, leaving more routine jobs for the times when your energy is low. Try turning the chores that you regard as work into things that are fun to do: power-walk to the shops, for example; put on your exercise gear, play some music and treat the vacuuming like an aerobic work-out; bend and stretch when you hang out the laundry and put away groceries; turn your dust-busting session into a fat-busting one!

Start now!
The only way of getting anything done is to make a start, so start now!

Live by the calendar
Buy a calendar or year-planner and mark all of your important events and dates – birthdays, dinner dates, holidays and days off – on it. This will help you to make sure that you never have to cancel dates with friends or family because all of your clothes need laundering!

Use a notebook
Buy a notebook and use it to make both a working list and a daily diary – let it take the place of all of those scraps of paper that are littering your home or handbag. As your year-planner indicates the approach of an important date, write it in your notebook, along with all of the things that you need to do or buy to make that date or event successful.

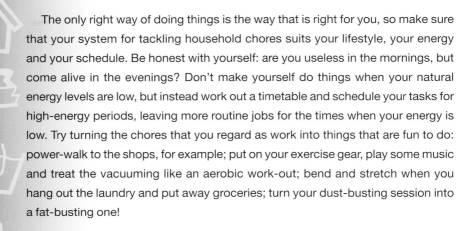

Details are important

Make sure that you write down all important telephone numbers, addresses, contact names and reference numbers in your notebook so that you have them to hand if you need them in a hurry. There's no need, for instance, to keep the box that your printer cartridge came in if you've already written down the cartridge's details. Take your notebook with you when you go shopping so that you can quickly refer to it.

Plan ahead

At the end of each week, plan your jobs for the week to come. That way you can slot small jobs into your busy schedule and complete them before turning to the more important things in life. Don't overlook the jobs that you hate: do one horrible, but necessary, job each day and get it over with!

If you're good for nothing in the morning, then get things ready the night before: lay out your clothes for the next day, pack your gym kit, lay the breakfast table, make your lunch, organise your bag or briefcase, make sure that your keys and money are to hand and perhaps transfer any coins that you've accumulated during the day into a jar each night so that you always have change for the bus to work. It doesn't take long to get organised, and you'll find that you're in less of a rush in the morning, giving you time to tidy up after breakfast so that you'll enjoy a more pleasant homecoming at the end of the day.

Keep a record

When your notebook is full, don't throw it away until you have gone through it and have transcribed all of the important entries – telephone numbers, addresses and any useful bits of information that you've accumulated – into a new notebook.

Make a separate inventory listing all of your valuables and noting down their serial numbers. A concertina folder is a good place in which to keep guarantees, records of dates of purchase and instruction booklets for household appliances,

and if you own a car, its ownership details and insurance certificates. In fact, try to keep any important documents in an orderly manner because if you lose them, they can be difficult to replace.

When time is money

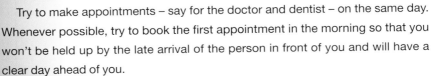

If we were paid for the time that we spent standing in queues at post offices, banks and supermarket checkouts, we'd be significantly wealthier! And time spent queuing is time that could be spent on more valuable activities. Using your notebook, plan to do errands when traffic is light and queues are short: Monday lunchtimes mean long queues at post offices and banks, but Tuesdays are quieter, for example.

Try to make appointments – say for the doctor and dentist – on the same day. Whenever possible, try to book the first appointment in the morning so that you won't be held up by the late arrival of the person in front of you and will have a clear day ahead of you.

Take your notebook with you, and if you happen to pass a shop that stocks something that your notebook tells you you'll need later in the week, nip in and buy it there and then to save yourself a future errand.

A place for everything

Most people complain that there is not enough storage space in their homes. In reality, there's often plenty of room, it's just that it's full of unused stuff. If you think that you won't be able to rustle up a meal unless your fridge and kitchen cupboards are full, for instance, chances are that you are wasting food and money. Have you opened and partially used two jars of the same spice? Are some packets of foodstuffs in your cupboards empty? Are you hoarding items that have passed their 'best by' or 'sell by' dates?

If your wardrobe and drawers are so full of clothes that you don't know what you've got, or you keep finding items that could only be worn to a 'really bad-taste fancy-dress party', you need to rationalise your storage space. In short, if you

don't know exactly what's stored in a cupboard or drawer in your home, it's time for a clear out to free up some of that valuable space.

Clearing the clutter

Clutter usually consists of items that are in the wrong place, so remember to store individual bits of sports kit together, to return coffee cups to the kitchen and to keep scissors, sticky tape and pens in one place so that you know where to find them.

From time to time, it's a good idea to go through your home room by room, clearing out any items that you don't want or that are worn out or broken. Start by clearing things from the floor and around the room, but don't dive straight into cupboards or wardrobes because you'll only make the room even more of a mess and will depress yourself. Put the items that you've cleared up into a large box. (If you have room mates, no matter how much you hate their tacky holiday souvenirs, don't throw them out without permission!)

When you've collected all of your unwanted clutter, go through the box and sort the contents into piles. Clean, wearable, cast-off clothes can go to the charity shop, along with books that you've either never read or will never read again. Torn or worn-out clothes can still be useful if you remove their buttons and zippers to use for repairs. Think creatively about their materials and fabrics, too, because if you enjoy sewing or knitting, you could use these fabrics to make a patchwork quilt or could unravel woollen jumpers and reuse the wool.

If you come across something in your box of clutter that you're not sure about, put it to one side. If you no longer care for an ornament or picture, but a friend admires it, give it to them. Remember, too, that there's often some money to be made from 'junk', so consider selling any unwanted items at a car-boot or table-top sale and use

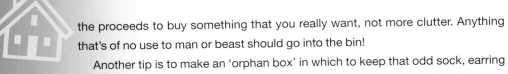

the proceeds to buy something that you really want, not more clutter. Anything that's of no use to man or beast should go into the bin!

Another tip is to make an 'orphan box' in which to keep that odd sock, earring or unidentifiable plastic bit that came with the stereo. If you later find the other sock or earring, then the pair can be sent to their rightful place, but if not, you can safely throw out the lone item. If you share your home with friends or family, dump any objects that have been left lying around in the 'orphan box', and if the culprit asks you where something is, just point at the box – they'll eventually get the message that they should tidy up their stuff!

Action stations

If you are to look after your home properly, you will have to invest in some essential equipment. Although there is a huge range of colourful buckets, brooms and other household items available, colour co-ordinating your cleaning kit will cost more than if you were to buy some more simple, functional items. Check out supermarkets and DIY superstores for special offers and compare their prices with independent hardware shops.

Buy a plastic storage box in which to store smaller items, and if you live in a large house that has a lot of stairs, it may be worth investing in two sets of cleaning tools so that you won't have to carry one set up and down the stairs. Finally, remember that however much you spend, it is important to keep your cleaning equipment clean!

Brushes and brooms

You'll need a long-handled broom, a hand brush and a dustpan. Before buying them, check that brooms and brushes are solidly made and that the tufts are firmly packed into smooth beech-wood or plastic heads. A broom should have stiff bristles with which to brush up loose debris from carpeted floors, while a softer brush should be used for hard floors, such as

wood or vinyl, and for dusting cornices, window ledges and coving. After use, clear the bristles of any loose particles by moving your hand across them. A great way of cleaning brushes and brooms in winter is to sweep them through clean snow a couple of times.

If your dustpan is slightly damp, you'll find that dust and floor sweepings stick to it and won't keep blowing away as you sweep.

Don't discard old toothbrushes or nailbrushes because these are ideal for cleaning fiddly areas – around kitchen and bathroom taps, for example.

Mops and buckets

You'll need at least one bucket, but two are better, especially if you are tackling jobs that involve cleaning and then rinsing with fresh water. If your budget won't stretch to a mop, an old T-shirt tied around a broom handle will work just as well.

Choose a bucket with a pouring lip, which makes disposing of waste water a lot easier. Some buckets are cylindrical, while others are more oval in shape, and make sure that you can place the mop head in the bucket without overturning it! Mop buckets with drainer attachments are sold for use with cloth mops, which were traditionally made of soft, cotton 'string', and although these are still available, they are best used for dry-dusting floors (note that until they are well broken in, they will shed fibres); such mop heads are today more usually made of strips of absorbent fabric. Sponge mops incorporating a lever with which to squeeze out excess water from the foam head can be expensive, but if you buy one, choose a model that takes replacement heads because these soon wear away.

Mopping a kitchen or bathroom floor does not mean soaking it in water: the mop head must be wrung out so that it is just damp enough to clean the floor. When you have finished, rinse out the mop

head until you have removed all of the dirt and the rinsing water runs clean.

If you use a dry mop with which to collect dust from floors, when you have finished, place a plastic or paper bag around the head and secure it with a twist tie – pipe cleaners are ideal (and can also be used for keeping electrical flexes in tidy bundles when appliances are not in use) – or rubber band. Then give the mop head a really good shake and discard the bag containing the dust.

Don't return mops to storage cupboards while they are still damp because they will make everything smell fusty. Instead, stand the mop on its handle outside, allow the mop-head strands to separate and leave them to dry. If you don't have access to an outdoor space, stick the mop head out of the window and gently pull the window onto the handle to hold it in place while the mop head dries.

Cleaning cloths

You'll need a selection of cloths for both wet and dry cleaning. If they are to clean efficiently, the cloths themselves need to be kept clean, so make sure that you buy ones that are soft, strong, absorbent, colour-fast and preferably machine washable. If you want to save money – and also be ecologically sound – avoid using disposable cleaning cloths and paper towels.

Don't throw away old T-shirts because these make fabulous soft dusters, while at last there's a use for that odd sock: slip it over your hand and dampen it slightly, and you've got a handy duster that is ideal for shelves and window ledges, as well as those difficult-to-access nooks and crannies.

Rubber gloves

Cleaning can be rough on your hands: hot and cold water, detergents and chemicals, dust and dirt can all take their toll on your skin and nails. Many cleaning agents furthermore contain substances that can irritate the skin, making it sensible to wear rubber gloves whenever you can. Remember, however, that the insides can become dirty and sweaty, making any existing skin or nail problem worse, although sprinkling a little talcum powder inside the gloves before putting them on will often help. Rubber gloves come in different sizes, and it's a good idea to wear ones that are a little too big for you to enable air to circulate around your hands.

If you are tackling a long cleaning job, try wearing a pair of thin cotton gloves (available from chemists) inside the rubber ones. If you buy a couple of pairs, you can reserve one for pampering your hands at the end of the day: before going to bed, put on some of your favourite hand cream, slip on your gloves and let the cream work its magic overnight.

Detergents and cleaning agents will corrode rubber gloves, so if one wears out, turn the other, entire glove inside out and wear it on your working hand.

After using rubber gloves, turn them inside out and let them dry out completely before wearing them again.

Cleaning products

Supermarket shelves are positively groaning under the weight of cleaning products – for floors, walls, windows, tiles, sinks and stoves – whose manufacturers would like us to believe are both essential and superefficient. Economy and supermarket own brands are both cheaper and usually as good, however, while buying larger sizes or splitting the cost of 'two for one' offers with a friend can save you even more. There's no need to buy a product to fulfil every advertised purpose because a basic cleaning kit consisting of washing-up liquid and a general-purpose cleaner will usually suffice. The type of general-purpose cleaner that you should buy will depend on the type of surfaces in your home: if they are easily scratched, for instance, you'll need a non-abrasive cleaner that is suitable for a range of surfaces.

There is also a whole range of inexpensive, readily available kitchen and DIY products that are not only efficient cleaners, but are probably already residing in your cupboards. Lemon juice, bicarbonate of soda (the baking soda used in cooking) and white-wine vinegar are just a few of the natural cleaners that are wonderfully effective when it comes to removing stains, grease and smells.

- Lemon juice can be used either neat or diluted to clean tarnish from brass and copper, to remove lime scale, rust and stains from marble and plastic worktops, to clean chopping boards and to rid microwave ovens of lingering food odours.

- White-wine vinegar can be used either neat, in a dilute solution with water or in a paste mixed with domestic (laundry) borax and water. In liquid form, white-wine vinegar cuts through grease and is an ideal cleaner for windows, mirrors and ceramic tiles; used neat, it will remove hard-water deposits from lavatory bowls and sinks, while a paste can be smeared around taps.
- Bicarbonate of soda is a mild alkaline that will neutralise acidic stains, such as those caused by fruit juice. Sprinkle a little onto a damp cloth for a gently abrasive cleaner that is also a natural deodoriser, making it ideal for cleaning fridges, freezers, ovens and microwaves, as well as china and stainless steel.

Certain surfaces and some particularly stubborn stains and marks need a little more specialised treatment, however, and although many branded products are designed to deal with these, it is often possible to treat them with a less glamorous alternative.

Household ammonia, which should always be used in a solution with water (wear rubber gloves, avoid it coming into contact with your skin, eyes and clothes and don't sniff the bottle – it smells disgusting!) is good for use on glass surfaces and ceramic tiles, as is methylated spirits (but note that meths is highly flammable and very poisonous).

Domestic, or laundry, borax softens water and breaks down grease. You can use it either in a paste with water and vinegar or diluted with water for cleaning enamel surfaces and ceramic tiles and for dissolving grease in sinks and drains. If you have sensitive skin, make sure you that wear protective gloves when using borax because it can cause irritation.

White spirit, a turpentine substitute, can be used to clean the gilt on items like picture frames and mirrors, as well as gently to remove layers of wax polish that have built up over time. You can also use it to dissolve rust spots on acrylic sinks and bathtubs, but remember that it is both poisonous and highly flammable and take care when working with it.

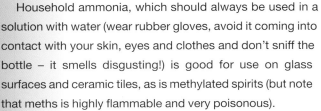

Washing soda also softens water and breaks down grease. Used in a hot-water solution, it will clean hard floors, cooker hoods, extractor fans and drains and will remove the green corrosion found on copper and brass, too. Again, make sure that you wear protective gloves when working with washing soda, and also ensure that you are using washing soda (sometimes called water-softener or powdered lime-scale remover), and not washing-soda crystals, which can react with some substances, particularly aluminium, causing noxious fumes.

CLEANING SAFETY: DO'S, DON'TS AND NEVERS

- Regardless of which cleaning products you choose to buy and use:
- Do follow the manufacturer's advice and warnings.
- Do protect your skin: wear protective gloves when handling products and when cleaning.
- Do store all cleaning products in a safe place out of reach of children and pets.
- Do dispose of used cleaning cloths and empty containers carefully and sensibly. Cloths soaked with turpentine, white or methylated spirits will remain flammable after use.
- Do wash your hands after using any cleansing agent, even if you have worn rubber gloves.
- Do watch your step! Sometimes you'll need to climb a ladder to reach areas that are hard to get at. Never over-reach yourself on a ladder. Never stand on a chair or table to reach anything, but instead use a stepladder or stool.
- Don't leave children alone with cleaning products, not even to answer the phone or doorbell.
- Don't mix cleaning products: some chemicals may react adversely if mixed, creating toxic fumes. If one product fails to do its job, wash the surface or item to which you applied it with water before using another.

- Never transfer household cleaners to other containers. If you do feel that you have to decant a cleaning product from a large container into a smaller one for ease of use, however, never use a container that has been used for drinks and always label the new container clearly, also including any of the manufacturer's warnings or instructions.
- Never use flammable products near a naked flame (including the pilot light on your oven or in your boiler). To avoid being overcome by fumes when cleaning, open as many windows as is practicable to provide adequate ventilation.
- Never clean electrical appliances without unplugging them first. Water and electricity are a lethal combination! Never operate any electric appliance, such as a vacuum cleaner, when your hands are wet, and take extra care when cleaning around socket outlets and light fittings.

SPIT & POLISH: CLEANING YOUR HOUSE

Keeping your home clean needn't be a heavyweight job, and the best way of avoiding it becoming one is to prevent dirt, dust and grime from building up by cleaning up spills when they occur, for example, or by washing up dirty dishes at once rather than letting them accumulate in the sink until you run out of clean cups and crockery. Quickly wiping over surfaces from time to time means that they won't become so dirty that they are really hard to clean later on. If you love your home, and cherish the things in it – the things that you worked so hard for in the first place – then caring for them becomes more of a pleasure than a chore.

A good starting point is to work out a once-a-week cleaning plan. This doesn't have to be written in stone, but if you follow your plan, you'll find that your home is pleasant to come home to in the evenings and that major cleaning tasks are kept to a minimum.

ORDER IN THE HOUSE

Start by opening the windows to let out the stale air and picking up anything that has been left lying around – yesterday's newspapers, junk mail, that out-of-date TV guide, anything in the waste paper basket – and either restore it to its rightful place or throw it out. Flowers that have wilted and faded and would need a miracle to revive them should also be thrown out: wrap them in some newspaper before putting them in the bin and dispose of the smelly water by pouring it down the lavatory (never pour the water down the kitchen sink because it is teeming with bacteria). If you are a smoker, empty all of your ashtrays and check that there are strikeable matches in any matchboxes rather than sticks of burnt wood.

Once a week, plan to vacuum your carpets, upholstery and curtains and to clean window surrounds, that is, their ledges and frames. Dust and polish furniture and give the tops of doorframes and skirting boards a wipe-over as well. In the bedroom, strip off the bedding, air the mattress and then vacuum it, paying particular attention to the indentations around the tops of the springs, before turning it over and vacuuming the other side. This will not only keep your mattress cleaner, but will even out the wear. (A friend once advised me never to sleep in the hotel bed that was nearest the telephone:

Impose order by clearing away the clutter littering your house and return things to their rightful places.

because guests sit on the edge of this bed when speaking on the phone, the mattress tends to dip more on one side.) This basic cleaning plan should help you to keep your home looking neat, tidy and

welcoming. Partly for the sake of hygiene, and partly because of their surface finishes, kitchens and bathrooms often require a little more energy expenditure to keep clean, however (see pages 65 to 84).

CLEANING AND MAINTAINING FLOORING

- House cleaning always starts at the bottom, with the floor. Whether you have fitted carpets, lino or vinyl, wood, tiles, marble or concrete flooring, this is where you'll find most of the dirt and grime because it's been carried from outside into your home on people's shoes. Sweeping and vacuuming regularly will not only cut down on heavy cleaning tasks, but will extend the life of your flooring (fragments of grit will scratch painted, waxed and varnished floors and will become embedded in the base of the tufts that make up carpets and rugs, where they can wear away the carpet fibres).

Sweep or vacuum hard floors a couple of times a week. This will prevent them being scratched by tiny particles of grit.

Hard floors

- Sweep or vacuum hard floors every few days and pay particular attention to corners because this is where dirt, grit, hairs (human and pet) and the odd paperclip will accumulate. Follow this by running a damp mop over sealed floors: using a low concentration of mild detergent in lukewarm water (if the water is too hot, it may damage any finish or polish on the floor), lay it on the floor with a clean mop and then pick it up again with a clean mop a few minutes later. (Make sure that you use clean mop heads to avoid leaving a fine film of dirt on the floor.)

- Where necessary, use a floor polish that is right for your floor to give it a good shine. There are three sorts of polish: solid pastes (for example, wax), liquid-solvent waxes (known as liquid waxes) and water-based emulsion waxes. Note that although you can use water-based emulsion waxes on most types of hard flooring, apart from unsealed wood and cork, the other two types of wax can only be used on certain floors.

Make your own floor polish

It is very easy to make a wonderful beeswax polish. You'll need some real beeswax – which resembles a small bar of yellow soap and is readily available – and some turpentine or turpentine substitute. Using the coarse side of a grater, grate a bar of beeswax, transfer the grated beeswax to a jar (with a screw-top lid), add just enough turpentine to cover the wax, screw on the lid and leave it for two days. Then shake the jar well and stand it in a bowl of hot water until it forms a paste. It is now ready for use. Apply it to wooden floors and furniture with a soft cloth.

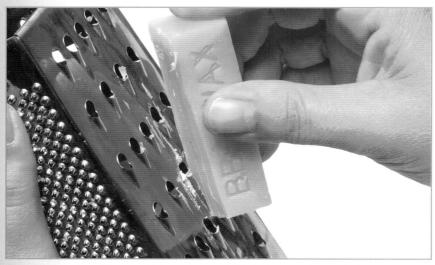

A bar of beeswax grated and then covered in turps makes a wonderful polish for wooden floors and furniture.

HARD-FLOOR TYPES AND TREATMENTS

Cork

Sweep a cork floor regularly and mop it with a solution of warm water and household detergent. Don't let the cork become too wet, however, because it may crack and crumble when it dries.

Plain cork can be sealed or polished: if it is polished, use a wax polish from time to time to give it a bit of shine, but don't use too much because the polish can build up and become very slippery.

Linoleum

Based on linseed oil, finely ground cork and wood 'flour' mixed with mineral fillers and bound on a hessian backing, linoleum once became a somewhat unfashionable floor covering, especially when trends in interiors favoured fitted carpets. With the advent of vinyl flooring, it seemed that lino had had its day, but as a result of the fashion for period restorations and interior styles, lino has made something of a comeback, and is today available in sheet or tile forms.

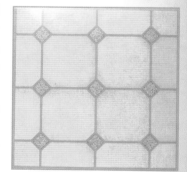

If you have a lino floor, you can wash it with warm, soapy water, but don't scrub it and instead remove any stubborn marks by gently rubbing them with a ball of medium-grade steel wool dipped in turpentine. Dry the floor thoroughly after cleaning it.

You can seal a lino floor to make maintaining it easier, but you will need to use an oil-based sealer, which will bond better than a plastic one. Old linoleum can often be revived by mopping it with a mixture of equal parts milk and turpentine and then rubbing it with a soft, warmed cloth.

Vinyl

Vinyl is an easy flooring to care for, and will last for a long time if it is well maintained. It needs regular sweeping and, when it is dirty, a wash with a warm-water solution of household detergent followed by a rinse with clean water. Don't use solvent-based cleaners on vinyl because they may strip off its protective surface, but you can use an emulsion polish to remove any

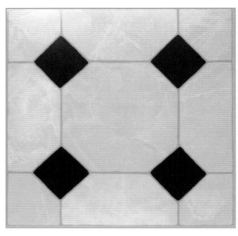

stubborn marks. When you wash adhesive vinyl floor tiles, try to keep your mop as dry as possible to prevent moisture from getting between the seams, which could eventually cause the corners of the tiles to curl.

When they are dry, vinyl floors can be coated with the manufacturer's recommended protective top dressing.

Ceramic tiles

Although ceramic tiles are tough and hard-wearing, beware of dropping any heavy objects onto them because they are liable to break, and can also be treacherously slippery when wet.

✳ ✳

Clean ceramic-tiled floors and surfaces with a solution of washing-up liquid applied with a sponge-headed mop or cloth, after which you'll need to wipe over the surface with a chamois leather. The grout between the tiles should be cleaned with a soft-bristled brush – an old nailbrush or toothbrush is ideal – dipped in either a strong solution of household detergent or a solution consisting of 1 part household bleach to 20 parts water.

Quarry tiles

Quarry tiles are first laid on a cement bed and then grouted, but unless they are sealed, they will remain porous. Newly laid quarry tiles shouldn't be washed for at least two weeks, although you could treat them to a light covering of linseed oil. Any white patches – known as efflorescence – caused by the lime in the cement can be washed away with a weak solution of vinegar and water: use 60 ml (about 4 tablespoons) vinegar to 5 litres (about 5 quarts) water and don't rinse it off afterwards.

Quarry tiles are usually coloured and are maintained with a red polish. Faded tiles will require rubbing with steel wool dipped in turpentine to remove any old residue prior to the repolishing process. You'll need to buff up the new polish to prevent it from sticking to shoes and being trodden into the flooring all over the house.

Wooden floors

Sanded and sealed floorboards only need sweeping or vacuuming and then a light mopping with a solution of household detergent. The seal will eventually begin to wear off, however, especially in areas of heavy traffic, such as doorways, and it's best to give these areas another sealing coat immediately, otherwise you'll end up having to strip the whole floor in order to reseal it completely.

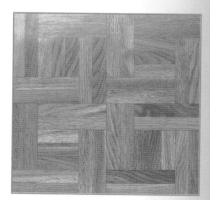

To avoid the wood swelling and warping when it dries out, never soak wooden floors. Don't wash them with very hot water either because this will make the wood soft and pulpy. Polished wooden floors shouldn't be washed at all, and you should instead use a proprietary liquid wax, which will clean and polish at the same time.

One old housekeeping tip is to sprinkle damp tea leaves onto wooden floors, which will help you to pick up the dust when sweeping. (Throwing tea leaves onto the floor also prevents dust and pollen from rising, making this an especially useful tip for people with allergies.) If you don't drink tea, coffee grounds work just as well, as do fresh cut grass clippings, which have the added bonus of smelling delightful.

Avoid scratching wooden floors when moving furniture by sliding the furniture over rugs or dressing the legs in old socks. To prevent rocking chairs from scratching the surface of wooden floors, glue a long strip of felt to the underside of each rocker arc.

Damp tealeaves sprinkled onto wooden floors help to collect dust and dirt, making cleaning quick and easy.

Removing stains and marks from hard floors

Stains caused by oil and grease can sometimes be removed from hard floors by mixing up a paste of fuller's earth with soap and water, applying the paste to the stain and leaving it there for two or three days. Although the paste is absorbent and will draw out the grease, you may have to repeat the process a couple of times, rubbing gently between each application, to get rid of the mark completely.

✳ ✳

To remove a scuff mark from vinyl, first try rubbing it with a pencil rubber. Alternatively, wipe the scuff firmly with a dry cloth to which you've applied a small amount of toothpaste. If that doesn't shift it completely, dab a tiny bit of turpentine onto a soft cloth and rub the mark gently.

To remove burns and scorch marks from vinyl, try rubbing them gently with a piece of fine abrasive paper. Fill small scratches and indentations with clear nail varnish, which you should apply in a series of thin coats, letting each coat dry thoroughly before applying the next.

Marks on vinyl can be removed with a pencil eraser.

Scratches on wooden floors can be dealt with by first rubbing them with some fine steel wool (avoid extending the rubbed area any further than is absolutely necessary), mixing a little brown shoe polish with some floor wax and rubbing it in well, so that the repaired area blends in with the surrounding floor.

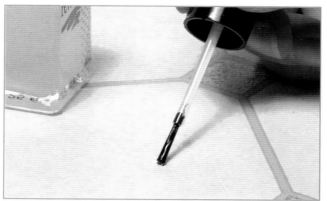

Clear nail polish is ideal for repairing small dents and scratches in vinyl.

CARPETS AND RUGS

Carpets and rugs are often the most expensive pieces of furnishing in a room, and although we expect them to last forever, we treat them very badly: food and drink spillages, cigarette ash, pet hairs and, of course, dirt carried in on shoes from outside all end up at the base of the tufts of their fibres.

CAUTION

Before using any type of carpet treatment, test a little of it first on an inconspicuous area to determine the carpet's colour-fastness.

Carpet maintenance and cleaning

New carpets shouldn't be vacuumed for four to six weeks after they have been laid to give the pile time to bed down. If the carpet is in a room that is subject to little traffic – a spare bedroom, perhaps – then leave it for even longer before vacuuming it. Once the pile has settled, vacuum the carpet regularly to remove any dust and dirt and to keep the pile in good condition.

Professional cleaners say that for a thorough sweep, a vacuum cleaner should be passed over each area of carpet at least eight times. If the carpet is loosely fitted, turn it over where possible and vacuum the reverse side as well. On fitted wall-to-wall carpets, use all of those attachments that came with your vacuum cleaner to get right into the corners. If your vacuum cleaner breaks down and you have to brush a carpet by hand, however, lightly sprinkle some damp salt over it first to prevent the dust from rising.

Slightly damp salt sprinkled lightly over carpets stops dust rising when sweeping by hand.

✳ ✳

Keep the vacuum cleaner's bristles clean and free of dust and fibres. Make sure that you have switched off and unplugged the vacuum cleaner before combing out the bristles – a wire dog comb is perfect for this task!

SOME FURTHER TRICKS OF THE TRADE.

- A room will look much neater if the fringed edges of rugs and runners are combed out with a wide-toothed comb (this is a useful way of quickly smartening up a room if visitors drop by unexpectedly!)
- Add a pleasant fragrance to your room at the same time as vacuuming it by placing a pad or ball of cotton wool soaked in eau de cologne or an aromatic oil in the vacuum cleaner's bag.
- Tape a bag to the side of the vacuum cleaner so that you can easily dispose of any larger items – bits of gravel or paperclips, for example – that you may pick up while vacuuming to prevent them from being sucked into the machine's innards.
- Carpets comprising man-made fibres tend to build up static and attract fluff. The easiest way of collecting this fluff is to dampen an old pair of nylon tights with warm water and then to wipe them over the carpet. To reduce the problem in the first place, mix 1 tablespoon of fabric softener with 6 tablespoons of water and then, using a plant sprayer, lightly spray the liquid over the carpet before allowing it to dry.

Harness static electricity to remove fluff, animal and human hairs stuck to carpets.

Dents in wool carpets caused by furniture and heavy objects can be cured by raising the pile. Place an ice cube on the dent, let it melt, leave the wet area to dry naturally and then vacuum it.

Carpet-cleaning

Thanks to dry-foam carpet shampoos, it's no longer necessary to make a carpet wet in order to clean it. Dry-foam carpet shampoos may dampen a carpet, but as the foam dries it crystallises and absorbs the dirt – at least in theory. These shampoos, which are sold in cans, are ideal for spot-cleaning small areas. If a whole carpet, or even a small, but valuable, oriental rug needs cleaning, you may have to hire specialised equipment, however, or, better still, call in a professional, but make sure that they are qualified and insured! (For advice, information and a list of registered carpet-cleaners in your area, contact the National Carpet Cleaners' Association – see end of book.)

A huge range of proprietary stain-removers and spot-cleaning kits for household use is also available for carpets and upholstery. These may either be general cleaners or those designed to tackle specific stains, so always follow the manufacturer's advice and instructions closely.

Alternatively, you may like to try some of the following tried-and-tested 'dry-cleaning' methods.

A quick way of brightening up a dull carpet is first to mix together 4 tablespoons of baby talcum powder, 3 tablespoons of cornflour (cornstarch) and 1 cup of bicarbonate of soda (baking soda). Sprinkle a thin layer of this mixture over the carpet, leave it overnight and then vacuum it off the next day.

A liberal sprinkling of bicarbonate of soda (baking soda), left on a carpet for half an hour before vacuuming, not only cleans the carpet, but neutralises unpleasant odours and discourages pests.

To remove loose dirt and dust from rugs, take them outside and beat them on their reverse sides with either an old tennis racket or a thin bamboo cane.

If you wake up to a snowfall, make the most of it by laying a rug face down in a patch of fresh, clean snow. Beat it thoroughly and then shake off any loose snow before letting the rug dry off completely.

Emergency measures

The trick to avoiding carpet stains is speed: the sooner you catch the stain, the better, but if your first treatment fails, let the carpet dry out completely before trying another strategy, which will give you a better idea of how much of the stain remains once the carpet is dry.

Here are some further tricks of the carpet trade.

If you've had a new carpet laid, keep any offcuts because they will be extremely useful in emergencies like this. If you rub a spare piece of carpet into the stained area when it is still damp, any colour that may have leached out of the carpet when you treated the stain will be restored.

Blot up liquid spills immediately with tissues. An old tip is to squirt the stain with a soda siphon or plant spray, and then to blot up the soda water with a clean cloth. Never rub or brush the stain, and remember to blot from the outside edge of the stained area to the middle.

If you don't notice a stain right away, or you don't want to embarrass a clumsy guest by immediately getting down on your knees to effect a remedy, let a diluted solution of white-wine vinegar, soap and water come to your rescue. Dampen a clean cloth with the solution and press – don't rub – it firmly against the stain for a few moments. Blot the area with clean cloth and then allow it to dry thoroughly before deciding whether an additional treatment is required.

Blot – don't rub – with a clean cloth to avoid spreading stains on a carpet.

A guide to common carpet stains and how to remove them

At some time in your carpet's life, one – or more – of the following substances will end up on it. If you act quickly, you may be able to repair the damage. If you have a proprietary stain-remover to hand, congratulate yourself! If not, don't panic because there are other rescue remedies available to you.

Beer

Blot up the spilt beer to absorb the excess liquid. Mix 10 ml (about 1 teaspoon) of washing-up liquid with 250 ml (1/2 pint) of lukewarm water. Apply the solution to the stain with a clean cloth and then blot it dry with a clean towel. For old beer stains, try a solution of 1 part white-wine vinegar to 5 parts water, followed by an application of clean water and then blot-drying. If that fails, try dabbing the stain with methylated spirits.

Wine

White wine causes less of a staining problem than red wine; clean it off carpets by blotting it with sparkling mineral water or soda water. Sadly, dealing with red-wine spills means that you'll have to waste some perfectly drinkable white wine. First soak up as much of the red wine as you can by blotting it with a dry, clean cloth, then place another clean cloth over the stain and pour some white wine onto it. Have a glass of white wine yourself while you wait for the stain to be soaked up, then blot the area dry and 'rinse' it by dabbing it with lukewarm water.

Red wine stains are easy to remove with white wine.

Coffee

Immediately spray the coffee stain with a soda siphon, or else blot it with a cloth dampened with clean, cold water. Follow this treatment by applying a mild detergent and then blotting the area dry with a clean towel. For dried-in stains, use a proprietary stain-remover.

Spilt coffee can be treated with soda water.

Tea

If the tea stain is still wet, glycerine will be the most efficient stain-remover: work it gently into the stain and then blot it with warm water. If the tea stain has dried in, apply some glycerine, leave it to soak into the stain and then clean it off by blotting it with water. Glycerine is sold by pharmacists, but if you don't have any to hand, try blotting the stain with lemon juice or white-wine vinegar.

Milk

Blot up as much of the milk as possible, rinse the stain with warm water, blot it dry and then leave it to dry thoroughly. It's the lingering smell that's the main problem with spilt milk, and if the odour lingers, either apply a neutralising carpet-deodoriser or liberally sprinkle over some bicarbonate of soda (baking soda) and leave it overnight before vacuuming it up.

The lingering smell of spilt milk is often worse than the stain. Bicarbonate of soda will remove the sour odour.

Curry

It's likely to be the turmeric – a spice commonly used in curries and pickles – that leaves a bright-yellow stain that's difficult to get rid of. When curry hits the carpet, you will need to use a proprietary stain-remover and will probably have to follow that with a shampooing as well. A large curry stain will need professional treatment.

Chewing gum

To remove chewing gum from your carpet, first hold a plastic bag filled with ice cubes over the area to harden the gum, then pick off as much as you can with your fingers. (This tip works for chocolate as well.) Any remaining chewing gum will need to be treated with a proprietary stain-remover.

Fat, grease and oil

Use brown or absorbent kitchen paper and a cool iron (see the treatment for candle wax above) to blot up as much fat, grease or oil as possible. Mixing fuller's earth or French chalk into a paste with water, dolloping the mixture onto the stain and leaving it to dry may absorb some of the residue (vacuum or brush up the mixture when it has dried). Any lingering spots may need treating with a proprietary stain-remover.

Candle wax

First scrape off any excess candle-wax deposits from the carpet. To remove the remainder, place a piece of brown paper, or absorbent kitchen paper, over the area and gently pass a cool iron over it. (Don't use the iron's steam facility and don't let it touch the carpet pile because it may scorch it.) Keep moving the paper around, or keep renewing it, as it absorbs the candle wax. Any small remaining residues can be dabbed with a little methylated spirits applied with a clean cloth.

While attractive when lit, candles can also be messy.

Use a cool iron over absorbent paper to gently melt and soak up wax stains.

Mud

Fresh mud stains can be treated with salt: sprinkle the salt liberally over the stain and let it soak up the moisture before vacuuming it off.

Shoe polish

Before doing anything else, carefully scrape off any excess shoe polish with a blunt kitchen knife, trying to avoid spreading the stain any further. The best treatment is a dry-cleaning solvent, but you could also try applying a little methylated spirits and then blotting the stain with clean water.

Soot

Soot can be problem if you have open fires in your home. The solution is to cover the soot with lots of dry salt and to leave it for half an hour before vacuuming it up.

Burns

Although burns are not strictly stains, sparks from cigarettes and open fires can still spoil a carpet, and can be lethal if they are not extinguished in time. If the burn is on a woollen carpet, immediately rub it with a slice of raw potato to remove the singeing on the surface. The

burnt brown tips of the carpet's tufts and fibres will sometimes come off if you blot them with a damp cloth. If they don't, try carefully trimming off the charred ends with a pair of nail scissors.

Ink

Tackle an ink stain immediately by blotting up as much of the ink as you can with some absorbent paper soaked in cold water – keep blotting to avoid saturating the carpet. Then form some more absorbent paper into a pad, soak it in a soap solution and leave it on the stain for 15 minutes. Repeat this process until all of the ink's colour has disappeared, blotting between applications. Although you have removed the ink's colour, you may still be left with a stain, particularly if the carpet is light in colour, in which case you'll need to use a proprietary stain-remover.

Tar

If a road surface is being relaid nearby, you can almost guarantee that some tar will stick to someone's shoe and will thus find its way into your home. Scrape off the

surface tar with a blunt kitchen knife and then blot the carpet thoroughly with a clean cloth dipped in oil of eucalyptus. (Oil of eucalyptus is by far the best remover of tar from fabrics, as well as from skin, so pack a bottle before going on holiday in case the beach is tarry.) When the tar has loosened, gently dab the side of a moistened bar of soap onto the stain and then blot it with a clean cloth soaked in fairly hot water. Repeat the procedure if necessary.

Blood

Sponge fresh bloodstains with cold water and then blot them dry. If the stain remains, you'll need to shampoo it. Dried-in stains require professional treatment.

Urine

Somewhat surprisingly, you can prevent a stain from forming if you treat a urine 'spill' before it dries. If a cat, dog or young child leaves a puddle on the carpet, spray either soda water or sparkling mineral water over the stain immediately. Mop up the liquid with a clean cloth, redampen the stain with soda or mineral water and then blot it again. If a cat is the culprit, giving the stain a final blot with some water to which 2 or 3 drops of ammonia have been added will discourage the feline from repeating its crime on the same spot. Before applying the ammonia solution to the stain, test it on an inconspicuous patch of carpet, however, because the ammonia may lighten some carpet dyes.

Vomit

Regardless of whether the source is animal or human, the only way to deal with vomit on carpets is to scoop up as much of it as you can and then to rinse the stained fibres with a solution of water and bicarbonate of soda before blotting it thoroughly and repeating the process until the stain has disappeared. As with milk spills, its often the odour that lingers, so try adding a few drops of antiseptic to the water that you'll be using to give the carpet a final rinse. If the odour remains, use a carpet-deodorising product.

✵ ✵

WALLS AND CEILINGS

Cleaning walls and ceilings is a big job, but fortunately one that needn't be tackled more than once a year. Most of the time, any cleaning of walls will be restricted to spots and marks that appear in areas of constant use, such as around light switches, at the sides of doorways and on walls next to staircases, where hands often touch or rest. Other marks may be made when furniture is moved, causing dents and chips in painted woodwork or torn wallpaper, or when your child one day decides to become an artist and creates murals in crayon all over the walls.

Don't bother trying to wash a dirty ceiling because it's better to paint it afresh in the long run. The appearance of most ceilings can, however, be improved by a good dusting: tie a clean duster around the head of a long-handled broom and get to work, shaking the dust from the duster from time to time to ensure that you're not just picking up and depositing the same dust.

If you are planning on redecorating, remember that the surfaces need cleaning first, before you paint or hang wallpaper.

Walls that are hung with non-washable wallpapers and other types of wall-covering should be dusted down with a dry duster. Never wash them because there is a risk that the colour will bleed and fade, causing the pattern to turn into a horrible grey mess and the wall-covering itself to come away from the wall.

The traditional method of removing marks from wallpaper is to rub a piece of white bread (crust removed) very gently over them. Be warned that you may need to use several slices of bread and that you must be gentle to avoid wearing a hole in the wallpaper. Alternatively, you could either buy a proprietary cleaning 'dough' (available from hardware shops) or make your own by mixing 100 ml (about 3 level tablespoons) of flour with 50 ml (about 1 1/2 tablespoons) of white spirit and 50 ml (about 1 1/2 tablespoons) of water, adding the liquids to the flour little by little and

then kneading the dough thoroughly. Rub the dough onto the affected area using a wide, sweeping movement, overlapping each area as you work. As the dough becomes dirty, turn it and mould it so that a clean section is facing the wall.

Because hands are inherently greasy, when they land on wallpaper they deposit grease and dirt. To remove a grease mark, place a piece of brown paper over the affected area and run a warm – not hot – iron across it. Repeat the procedure, each time moving a new, clean section of the paper over the grease mark, until all of the grease has been absorbed.

If an area of wallpaper is badly marked, it may be better to patch it rather than clean it. Do this by tearing off a matching piece of spare wallpaper, pulling away from it as you tear (although this will make an uneven edge, it will be less obvious than a neatly cut one). Stick the new patch into position with wallpaper paste, matching up the components of any pattern as best you can. To ensure that the colour of the new patch matches the older wallpaper, thus making a less conspicuous repair, leave the new piece in strong sunlight for a day or two until the colour has faded.

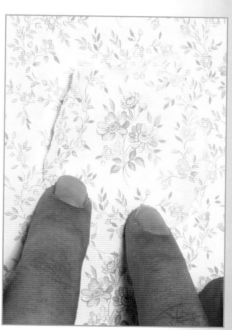

A torn replacement patch has softer edges and so is less visible when pasted over the damaged area.

Tear wallpaper away from you, so white 'edges' are less obvious.

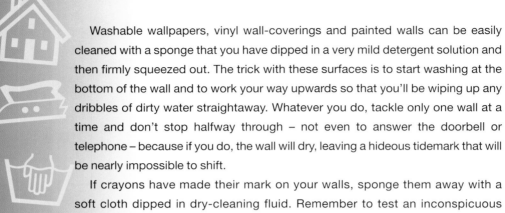

Washable wallpapers, vinyl wall-coverings and painted walls can be easily cleaned with a sponge that you have dipped in a very mild detergent solution and then firmly squeezed out. The trick with these surfaces is to start washing at the bottom of the wall and to work your way upwards so that you'll be wiping up any dribbles of dirty water straightaway. Whatever you do, tackle only one wall at a time and don't stop halfway through – not even to answer the doorbell or telephone – because if you do, the wall will dry, leaving a hideous tidemark that will be nearly impossible to shift.

If crayons have made their mark on your walls, sponge them away with a soft cloth dipped in dry-cleaning fluid. Remember to test an inconspicuous area of wallpaper for colour-fastness first, and if you find that the fluid has left a ring, you'd be better advised to use a paste made of fuller's earth, French chalk and cleaning fluid. Test the paste, too, and if the wall's colour doesn't bleed, smooth the paste over the crayon marks and let it dry completely before brushing it off.

Tackle doors and woodwork last, leaving skirting boards (often the dirtiest parts) until the very end. Painted woodwork can be washed down with a solution of water and washing-up liquid (don't use detergents because they can adversely affect paint colours), after which you should wash off the solution with clean water and then blot the woodwork dry with a clean cloth.

Walls that have been tiled with ceramic tiles should be cleaned the opposite way to other walls, that is, from top to bottom. If you want shiny, smear-free tiles, you'll need to polish them dry after you've washed and rinsed them with clean water. Spruce up ceramic tiles and give them some sparkle by rubbing them with half a lemon and buffing them dry.

Grimy grout is not only unsightly, but also unhygienic, so scrub it clean with an old toothbrush or nailbrush dipped in a mild solution of household bleach and water. Old grout can be spruced up with grout paint, which is available in a range of colours, enabling you to make your grout either co-ordinate or contrast with your tiles.

LET THERE BE LIGHT:
....

cleaning windows, glass and mirrors

The best time to clean the outside of your windows is on a dry, but dull, day in spring, or at least when the sun isn't shining on them because when it is bathed in sunshine, the glass will dry too fast, so that you'll end up with streaks. Don't clean windows on frosty days either because the extreme cold will make both the glass and putty brittle, increasing the danger of you either breaking your windows or pushing panes of glass out of their frames. (If you do break a window – or any piece of glassware, for that matter – pick up any fine slivers, splinters or fragments of glass by pressing a slice of white bread against them.)

Clean windows – and window frames – look and smell good. Take extra care up ladders though!

Here are a few more tips for cleaning windows, glass and mirrors.

Always clean the window frames before starting on the glass. (You can make your own windowsill cleaner by mixing 1 part rubbing alcohol with 8 parts warm water.)

Make sure that curtains are held well away from windows when washing them by looping the hems over a coat hanger and then hanging the coat hanger at the furthest end of the curtain pole or track.

If windows or mirrors are dusty or gritty, you'll need to wash the glass before cleaning or polishing it to prevent the tiny particles of dirt from scratching the glass.

Adding a dash of vinegar to clean water makes a terrific glass-cleaner: not only does it add sparkle, but it also wards off flies in hot weather.

✳ ✳ ✳ ✳ ✳ ✳ ✳ ✳ ✳ ✳ ✳ ✳ ✳ ✳ ✳ ✳ ✳ ✳ ✳ ✳

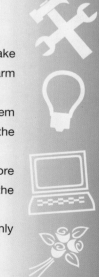

You can make a good window-cleaning solution by adding 5 ml (about 1 teaspoon) of household ammonia and 15 ml (about 1 tablespoon) of methylated spirits to 500 ml (about 1 pint) of water. To have it to hand, and for easy application, store it in a labelled plant-sprayer.

Note that proprietary window-cleaning solutions should be applied to dry windows because if the solution comes into contact with any moisture or condensation on the glass, it will spread around, making it difficult to remove and often resulting in smears.

You'll find it much easier to locate any stubborn smears if you dry one side of a pane of glass with horizontal strokes and the other with vertical ones.

Clean flyspecks off windows with hot water and a cleaning cloth to which you've added a dash of paraffin. Not only does this shift flyspecks faster than anything else (although other people swear by cold tea, it's never worked for me), it's also said to stop the flies from coming back.

The quickest – and cheapest – way of cleaning windows and mirrors is with a slightly damp, scrunched-up newspaper; dry and polish the windows or mirrors with more crumpled newspaper. Avoid using too much water, especially when cleaning mirrors because excess water may dribble down into the frame and attack the silvering on the back.

You can also deter flies from landing on window frames by rubbing the frames with either lavender oil or citronella (a lemon oil). Flies hate basil, too, so you could try hanging some basil leaves in the window or, better still, grow a pot of basil in the kitchen, where it'll be to hand when you want to flavour your cooking with this aromatic herb.

Reduce condensation on windows in cold weather by placing a saucer full of salt (which absorbs moisture) on the windowsill.

Stop your bathroom mirror and windows from steaming up by adding a few drops of glycerine to the rinsing cloth at the end of the cleaning process.

CURTAINS AND BLINDS

Condensation can form on windows in even in the best-ventilated houses, so it's always a good idea to hang curtains some way away from the glass to avoid them touching it. Lining curtains prevents their colours from fading in the sunlight and also stops any moisture on the windowpanes from damaging the curtain fabric. (If your curtains are lined, note that even though the fabric of both the curtains and their lining may be washable, they may shrink at a different rate in the wash.)

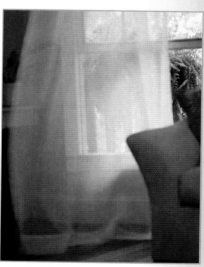

Curtains that are hung with a cording set – strings that you pull to open and shut the curtains – will last longer, especially if they are velvet, because your hand need never touch, and hence mark, the fabric. Vacuum your curtains regularly to keep them dust-free and cleaner for longer.

Window dressing: curtains and blinds finish a room but need care and attention to keep looking good.

Before washing any curtains, check that they have been preshrunk; if they haven't been, they may not fit your windows after you've washed, dried and rehung them. If you're not sure whether they have been preshrunk, it's best to have them dry-cleaned. (If you've used a coin-operated dry-cleaning machine before transporting your newly cleaned curtains home in a car, make sure that you keep at least one window open to enable any dry-cleaning fumes to escape rather than build up inside the car.)

If you decide to wash heavy curtains yourself, the best way to do so is to lie them in your bathtub one at a time; because they will be too heavy for your washing machine to handle, the appliance could end up damaged and the curtain fabric torn.

Before washing curtains, remove any hooks or rings, as well as any weights making them hang straight (mark their position on the curtain with a small dot of nail varnish so that you won't have to spend time later on working out where they once were).

If the curtains are large, or sunlight has damaged them, there is a danger that washing them may tear them into shreds at the fabric's weak points. If you have antique or fragile curtains, you may find the following cleaning method used by museums and conservators helpful. Fold each curtain into a manageable square or rectangle and use very long tacking stitches to sew the layers together. Rinse the curtains in clean water several times, then transfer them to lukewarm, soapy water and squeeze – don't wring – them. When the curtains are clean, rinse them under

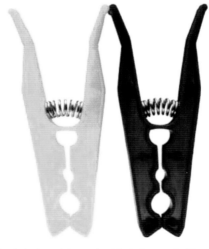

Use plenty of pegs to hang out curtains to dry so no strain is placed on the fabric.

✳ ✳

running cold water and squeeze them out gently. Unpick the tacking threads, carefully unfold the curtains and then hang them out to dry (use plenty of clothes pegs so that no strain is placed on the fabric). When the curtains are dry, fold them horizontally – not lengthways – and, finally, iron them. Iron curtains lengthways, gently stretching and pulling them into shape as you work to avoid the seams puckering.

Although lace curtains should be handled in the same way as fragile curtains, they are best dried by spreading them flat on a clean surface, such as a lawn, and leaving them to dry out slowly in the shade. If you must hang lace curtains on a line, lay them over the line so that they run down its length. Place a sheet of tissue paper over the fabric to prevent the iron's point from catching in the holes and then iron lace curtains with a cool iron.

Net curtains and voiles are usually made of nylon or polyester. These fabrics often yellow with age, but can be revived by washing them in a lukewarm solution of washing-up liquid. To make them really white, add a denture-cleaning tablet to the solution. Net curtains are best rehung while they are still quite damp, which will make it easier for you gently to pull them into shape.

While your curtains are down, take the opportunity to clean the poles and tracks, and remember to dust or vacuum any pelmets, both inside and out.

When you rehang a pair of curtains, it's advisable to reverse their original positions on either side of the window. This is because the edges that met when the curtains were drawn will have received the most wear and may have faded more at the outer edges, but by changing the curtains' positions, you can even out the wear and fading.

Slatted or Venetian blinds are notorious for collecting dust. Keep them clean by passing an 'L'-shaped wedge of bread along them. Another method is to slip an old sock, cotton glove or oven glove with a little fabric-softener sprinkled on it over your hand and then to run it along the slats. (The oven glove is the best option because its thickness means that you can clean both sides of the slats at the same time.)

If you are renewing a Venetian blind, consider buying one with vertical slats, the advantage of these being that they require less cleaning because dust has no horizontal surface to settle on.

Vacuum fabric roller blinds regularly, and don't forget to dust the roller springs as well.

Venetian blinds are easily dusted if you put an old sock over your hand.

SOFT FURNISHINGS AND UPHOLSTERY

Like all other fabrics, the more regularly you clean your soft furnishings and upholstery, the less the likelihood that they will need a major renovation. Dirt, dust, hairs – both pet and human – and hair preparations like gels and setting sprays, which can be deposited on chair and sofa backs, as well as smoke from cigarettes and fumes from cooking, will all eventually discolour and damage fabrics. Vacuum upholstered furniture every week and turn cushions from time to time so that they wear evenly.

Although there are numerous upholstery shampoos and cleaners on the market, before using one – or any other treatment, for that matter – on a piece of upholstered furniture, look for the care label (the furniture industry's standard cleaning code, which should be attached to all soft furnishings), which will tell you which cleaning method to use. It's also advisable to check the code if you intend to buy a new piece of upholstered furniture to ascertain whether it suits your needs and requires any special treatment.

THE MEANINGS OF THE CODE LETTERS ARE AS FOLLOWS:

W: this letter indicates that the upholstery should only be cleaned with a foam upholstery shampoo or other suitable water-based cleaner specifically designed for upholstery.

S: this indicates that a water-free dry-cleaning solvent should be used. This means that, apart from 'spot'-cleaning, it's best have to have the upholstery professionally cleaned.

S-W: this means that the upholstery should only be cleaned with an upholstery shampoo or a water-free solvent.

X: this indicates that the upholstery should only be vacuumed regularly and that no cleaning agents should be used.

Before treating any upholstery, remember to vacuum it first to remove as much loose dirt and dust as possible. Always check a very small, inconspicuous area of the fabric for colour-fastness by applying the upholstery shampoo, leaving it for a little while and then dabbing it with a clean tissue or paper towel. If no colour comes away on the tissue or towel, it's safe to proceed; if it does, call in the professionals.

Whichever product you use, always follow the manufacturer's instructions; treat a small area at a time; and use as little moisture as possible to avoid wetting the padding or stuffing.

Check a small area of fabric for colour-fastness before treating upholstery.

If you're using a dry-foam upholstery cleaner, you'll need to rub the foam well into the fabric; rub up and down, using overlapping strokes, and then across in the same way – don't rub in circles! These foam cleaners are normally supplied with an applicator brush, but if you find this too large to work with when tackling a small spot, use an old, clean toothbrush instead. Remember to remove the foam residue and loosened dirt afterwards and to allow the treated area to dry before vacuuming it again.

One effective upholstery-cleaner that is excellent for removing spots from Dralon velvet upholstery, as well as for removing shiny marks on upholstered armchairs caused by hands resting on their arms, is a clean cloth dampened with 1 dessertspoon of white-wine vinegar mixed in 250 ml (1/2 pint) of lukewarm water.

Animal hairs seem to be largely immune to vacuum cleaners, no matter how powerful they are. Here are some of the best ways of removing pet hairs from soft furnishings:

- slip on a rubber glove and rub your hand over the soft furnishings; doing this will cause the hairs to bunch together, making them easier to pick off;
- gently rubbing a sheet of fabric-softener over soft furnishings works well, but it is a more expensive method than most;
- by far the simplest method, as well as the cheapest, is to dampen a clean cloth slightly and then to rub it gently over the soft furnishings; as with the rubber-glove method, this will cause the hairs to cling together, making them easier to remove.

Cover the soft furnishings with adhesive tape and then rip it off; as you remove the tape, the hairs will come away, too.

Washable loose covers are easier to fit – and will fit better – after you have washed them if you put them back on the furniture while they are slightly damp (they will be more likely to dry in the correct shape this way). If the loose covers are a little creased when you have refitted them, simply iron them using a warm or cool iron (never use a hot iron because there is a danger that it could cause scorch marks, as well as any foam padding or stuffing to dissolve).

CARING FOR FURNITURE

You will need to care for leather, cane, wicker and wood furniture in different ways.

Leather furniture

Before attempting to clean any leather furnishings, always check the manufacturer's care instructions. Some leather furniture is made of dyed leather, which can be stained permanently, while other types are made of pigmented leather. To find out whether the leather is dyed or pigmented, carry out a water-droplet test by placing a single drop of clean water on an inconspicuous bit of the leather. If the water soaks in straightaway, then so will any stains; this is dyed leather, and you will need to call in the professionals. If the water doesn't soak in, however, the leather is pigmented, and you have a chance of removing certain stains. The general rule is that you should not wet leather too much; most water-based stains can in any case be removed up with a damp cloth.

A drop of water will soak into dyed leather. If it doesn't soak in, then the leather is pigmented.

Keep leather furniture away from heat sources like radiators, as well as intense direct sunlight, which will cause the leather to dry out. Dust leather furniture regularly; gently wipe over it with a soft, damp cloth; and give it an occasional 'feed' with hide food, which will prevent the leather from drying out and cracking, also discouraging stains. You can make a good leather-conditioner by mixing 2 parts boiled linseed or olive oil with 1 part white-wine vinegar. Shake the solution well, apply it sparingly with a damp cloth, let it dry and then buff the leather with a soft, dry cloth.

Wicker and cane furniture

To remove dust and dirt from their nooks and crannies, wicker and cane furniture need either regular dusting or vacuuming with a hose attachment.

Because most cane furniture has been given a light seal or varnish as a finish, don't scrub it too hard, however, or you'll end up scratching the surface. Wicker furniture is best cleaned by scrubbing it with warm salty water, which will both keep the wicker stiff and prevent it from yellowing.

As a result of their origins, wicker and cane like to be kept in a humid environment and will become dry and brittle if the atmosphere is too dry. Placing cane and wicker furniture outside during a heavy summer shower will revive them if this happens (but remember to bring such garden furniture inside during the winter because it can't tolerate really cold temperatures). Alternatively, if a wicker chair is looking a little dry and fragile, rub a little lemon oil into it.

You can scrub cane furniture from time to time with a mild solution of washing-up liquid, or some lemon juice and salt dissolved in warm water, and an old nailbrush.

Wooden furniture

Any modern, factory-made wooden furniture in your home will generally have been finished to protect it, while antique wood will need special care and attention.

The natural beauty of wood is often enhanced by a polished, waxed or varnished finish.

NUMEROUS FINISHES ARE GIVEN TO WOOD, FALLING INTO THREE MAIN CATEGORIES, AS FOLLOWS.

French polish: this is where the finish has been built up with layers of shellac dissolved in spirit to create a satin finish. French polish is easily scratched and marked by water, and repairs or restorations require skill and patience.

Lacquer or varnish: this accounts for the finish that is given to most of the modern furniture that we buy. It results in a very hard-wearing layer of lacquer or varnish that is designed to provide protection against bumps, heat and moisture and that is applied to either solid wood or to veneers (thin strips of wood, paper foil or plastic) covering the surface of less valuable, or attractive, woods and fibreboards. This finish doesn't need any additional protection, and a polish won't penetrate the varnish in any case, although it will give the surface some shine.

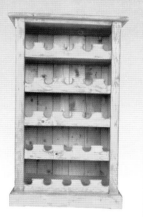

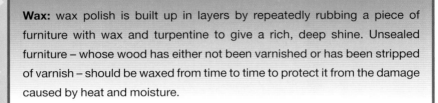

Wax: wax polish is built up in layers by repeatedly rubbing a piece of furniture with wax and turpentine to give a rich, deep shine. Unsealed furniture – whose wood has either not been varnished or has been stripped of varnish – should be waxed from time to time to protect it from the damage caused by heat and moisture.

Waxes and polishes that have been designed for wood will remove dirt and grease deposits and will enhance the wood's natural beauty by reflecting light off it. Here are some waxing and polishing tips to help you to care for your wooden furniture.

Pine furniture needs little more than a polish with a good beeswax polish. Once it has developed a pleasing shine, the piece need only be wiped over with a cloth dampened with equal amounts of vinegar and paraffin. To make your own beeswax polish, coarsely grate 50 g (2 oz) of natural beeswax, transfer it to a screw-top jar and add 150 ml (5 oz) of turpentine (not turpentine substitute). Screw the lid loosely on the jar and stand the jar in a bowl of hot (not boiling) water until the beeswax melts. Shake the jar until the mixture forms a paste and then let it cool. It's now ready for use, but if you find that the wax has become too hard when you next want to use it, stand it a bowl of hot water to soften it a little.

Beeswax is a common ingredient in many commercial waxes and polishes, but it can be bought easily to make your own.

Make a preparation with which to dust pine furniture speedily by putting small quantities of paraffin and vinegar in equal parts into a labelled, screw-top jar, popping in a clean duster, sealing the jar and waiting until the cloth has absorbed all of the liquid, when it will be ready to use. After use, return the cloth to the jar and screw on the lid tightly to ensure that it stays damp.

Make a wonderful polish for oak furniture by mixing together a small lump of melted beeswax, 500 ml (1/2 pint) of beer and 10 g (2 teaspoons) of sugar. Apply the polish with a soft paintbrush, leave it to dry and then buff it thoroughly with a chamois leather.

Revive dull ebony by applying some petroleum jelly and leaving it for about thirty minutes before wiping it off.

To give waxed furniture a shine, rub a piece of waxed kitchen paper over it before buffing it with a soft cloth.

Waxed furniture can be given a 'quick finish' by running a piece of waxed kitchen paper over the surface.

It's often easier to apply shop-bought polishes if you first dampen the cloth with a little water.

Don't apply wax to a dirty or dusty surface because you'll either seal in the dirt or dust or, even worse, move it around and scratch the surface of the furniture.

> Don't be heavy-handed when applying polish. Apply too much, and it will dry out and leave you with smears, making it difficult to buff up a shine.

Don't apply wax too frequently – once or twice a year is quite enough – because a build-up of wax will make the surface of the furniture sticky, thus attracting dirt. If, having waxed a piece of furniture, you run your finger across the surface and it smears, you've applied too much wax.

To remove a build-up of wax, first try wiping the wood with a cloth soaked in vinegar and warm water and then rubbing off the solution at once with a dry cloth. If this doesn't work, soak a clean cloth in white spirit and wipe the wood, working in the direction of the grain until all of the dirt and wax has been removed. Allow the wood to dry and then give it a wipe with a clean, dry cloth. The surface can now be rewaxed, but remember to use the wax very sparingly.

Treating marks on wood

When treating marks on wood, the golden rule is to tread carefully.

White rings and marks on wood – especially table tops – indicate that heat has damaged the finish. Run your fingers lightly over the ring or mark to ascertain the damage and treatment. If the surface has not been roughened, you may be able to burnish out the ring or mark by briskly rubbing in a little metal-polish cream (remember always to rub in the direction of the grain) and following this up with a light application of wax. If the surface feels rough, however, apply liquid wax with a ball of

very fine steel wool; don't scrub the wood, but instead work gently along the grain at little at a time, working with extreme caution if the surface wood is a thin veneer. Remember to test any proprietary ring-mark-removers on a hidden area before applying them to the ring mark.

To remove water marks caused by placing wet glasses or vases on wooden surfaces, spread mayonnaise over them, leave it on overnight and then wipe it off with a soft cloth. If you prefer, you could try following the instructions given above

for treating ring marks. Alternatively, if the water mark is small, try mixing a little petroleum jelly with some cigarette ash and rubbing this substance over the affected area.

Be warned that spilled grease will leave a dark stain on wood unless you treat it quickly. Blot up the excess grease with paper towels, dab some neat vinegar onto the

Mop up water from wooden surfaces as soon as possible to avoid making marks.

affected spot, which will cut through the grease, and then wipe the area with a cloth dampened in a solution of equal parts vinegar and warm water.

My final tip is that both peppermint oil and white toothpaste are good all-purpose stain-removers for wooden furniture!

Dealing with dents and scratches in wood

Dents in solid wood can sometimes be treated by being filled with hot water, which

can make the wood fibres swell up. If a dent occurs on a vertical surface, such as a table leg, cover the dent with damp blotting paper and apply a warm iron to the area.

Disguise minor scratches in wood by 'colouring in' with a wax crayon in a matching colour.

Scratches can be treated in the same way as dents, but if this fails, you can often disguise a scratch by rubbing it with a wax crayon of a matching colour (either a child's colouring crayon or one that has been specially designed for masking scratches in furniture). If you need a quick fix, masking a scratch with shoe polish, eyeliner or an eyebrow pencil of the same colour will do the same trick. Spreading a little cod-liver oil over the scratch and leaving it for twenty-four hours before polishing it off will often improve its appearance, and sometimes even make it disappear. Another scratch treatment that is often successfully used on dark-colored woods is to rub the cut edge of a brazil nut over the affected area.

Precious things

Here are some useful tips for looking after precious objects.

- The gilt frames of pictures and mirrors are best cleaned by dabbing – never rubbing – them with a soft cloth dampened with a mixture of equal parts ammonia and denatured alcohol, such as methylated spirits. Work on a small area at a time, then pick up the dirt with a soft, dry cloth. Twice a year, apply a tiny amount of lemon oil to prevent cracking.
- Dust oil paintings to remove any loose dust. A traditional method of cleaning them a little is to blot the surface with a piece of soft bread.
- Clean glass flower vases by filling them with hot water and dropping in a couple of denture-cleaning tablets.
- Clean ivory piano keys by rubbing them with either half a lemon or a paste made of lemon juice and salt before wiping them clean with a cloth. (Never use soap on ivory because it will cause staining.) Give plastic piano keys a brilliant shine by buffing them with white toothpaste applied to a soft cloth.
- Remove stains from marble with a paste made of bicarbonate of soda (baking soda), water and lemon juice. Then rinse and dry the marble.

- Damp is a book's worst enemy, so don't pack your books tightly together on shelves, but instead let the air circulate around them. Placing pieces of charcoal behind rows of books, in the space between them and the walls (which may be damp), will help to prevent books from becoming mildewed.

- If you drop a book in the bath – it does happen! – rescue it by placing tissues between each page to soak up the water. Let the book dry out before removing the tissues.
- Protect leather-bound books from developing spots of mould by rubbing the leather with lavender oil.
- A mixture of lemon and salt is traditionally used for cleaning brass items, but rubbing on some Worcestershire sauce or toothpaste with a soft cloth also works.

The mild, yet effective, citric acid in lemons makes an ideal brass cleaner.

Clean chrome with neat vinegar or nail-varnish remover, or else with some cold dregs of black tea.

Silver is the metal that is the most prone to tarnishing, a process caused by hydrogen sulphide in the atmosphere acting on the surface of the metal. Certain foodstuffs, notably salt, eggs, olives, fish, vinegar, fruit juices and even mushy peas, also encourage tarnishing because the acids that they contain etch themselves into the silver, causing pit marks. It's therefore important to wash any silver items that have come into contact with these foods as soon as possible after use with a warm solution of washing-up liquid, followed by a rinse in hot water, before drying the items. Never put silver in the dishwasher because dishwasher detergent causes black marks.

When cleaning silver, use a metal polish that has been specially formulated for it. These range from liquids and creams through wadding to impregnated cloths and dips. You also can make your own silver dip very easily. Line a plastic washing-up bowl with tinfoil, fill it with very hot water and add a handful of washing soda*. Immerse the silver object in the solution, making sure that it touches the tinfoil. (The cleaning process involves a chemical reaction that removes the tarnish from the silver and deposits it onto the tinfoil.)

Line a plastic washing up bowl with kitchen foil, fill with hot water and add a handful of washing soda to make a silver dip.

Don't overpolish silver: rubbing too hard can scratch the surface, and rubbing in circles makes marks.

Any large items that protrude above the water line will need to be turned after about five minutes, but don't leave any silver items in the dip for longer than ten minutes. When the foil has turned black, it has lost its power to collect any further deposits and will need changing.

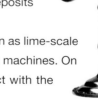

(*Outside North America, washing soda is often known as lime-scale remover or water-softener and is sold for use in washing machines. On no account use washing-soda crystals, which can react with the tinfoil, generating noxious fumes.)

Silver is a soft metal, and because a fine layer of the surface metal is removed every time a tarnished item is cleaned, it's important not to overpolish your silver. Not only can the abrasive action remove details over time, but rubbing too hard can also scratch the surface, so use straight, even strokes and don't rub crosswise or in circles.

ATMOSPHERICS

Here are some cunning ways of giving your home a fragrant atmosphere.

- Dipping candlewicks in vinegar and leaving them to dry will prevent them from smoking as they burn.
- Candles burn for longer if they are cold, so put them in the fridge before a dinner party.
- Don't discard the stubs and ends of scented candles, but instead store them in a small, thick, cotton bag. They will continue to give off their scent without melting if the bag is placed in a warm spot, such as sunny windowsill or an airing cupboard.
- Minimise the smell of cigarette smoke by discreetly positioning a saucer full of vinegar somewhere in the room.

- Burning charcoal absorbs the smell of stale cigarettes, as does cat litter (although this is admittedly a less attractive option!)
- Boiling a small pot of water to which you've added a few drops of vanilla essence or a cinnamon stick makes a wonderful room fragrance.
- If you have an open fire, give your room a citrus smell by burning some orange, lemon or grapefruit peel.
- Throwing coffee grounds on a fire will rid a room of any unpleasant smells. On the subject of coffee, the aroma of freshly ground coffee is always welcoming.

- Lavender bags are not just for wardrobes: hanging a bunch of lavender or mixed herbs, or else a small muslin bag stuffed with them, above a fireplace will produce a wonderful smell when the heat of the fire releases the herbs' aromatic oils.

The scent of burning coffee grounds is very inviting.

Lavender filled bags hung on clothes hangers not only make wardrobes smell wonderful, they also keep moths away from your clothes.

TIPS FOR THE BEDROOM

There are a number of things that you can do to keep your bedroom – and everything in it – fresh and clean.

- Throw back the bedcovers every morning. Because our bodies lose about 300 ml (1/2 pint) of moisture every night, your bed will require about twenty minutes to dry off each day before you remake it.

- Always remove the plastic covering from a new mattress; if you leave it on, your body will create condensation within it, leading to mildew.

- Because removing stains from a mattress is a tough job, it's better in the long run to fit your mattress with a washable, cotton mattress-protector.

- Either turn over your mattress or reverse the head and foot ends regularly – about every three months, but more often when it is new – to keep the stuffing even and distribute any wear. Foam mattresses, however, which generally have a layered construction, shouldn't be turned, but their head and foot ends instead reversed.

Sweet dreams: a pleasant bedroom is inviting and relaxing.

- You'll need to remove the accumulated dust and dead skin from your mattress regularly, too. Although you can use a vacuum cleaner on a light-suction setting for a foam mattress, it's best to brush sprung and other types of mattress to avoid dislodging the layers of padding beneath the mattress cover.

- Remake the bed before dusting the rest of the room to prevent any dust that you raise from settling on the mattress.
- Air your pillows by hanging them on a clothesline.
- Change your pillowcases regularly, and cover each pillow with two – or else one and a protective case – to prevent natural skin and hair oils and face creams from penetrating through to the stuffing.
- Don't put pillows in coin-operated dry-cleaning machines because the cleaning solvent's toxic fumes may become trapped within them, which may endanger your health.
- Pillows don't last forever, so treat yourself to a new one when the old one has worn out. If you plump up your old pillow, lay it across your outstretched arm and it then flops down at either side, it's time to replace it.
- It's essential to air duvets – regardless of their filling – daily. Drape them over a chair, the bed's foot rail or, even better, an outdoor clothesline to enable the flattened filling to expand and dry out.
- Don't keep sheets and pillowcases in heated airing cupboards for long periods because if you do, they will become marked and discoloured.
- Storing an electric blanket can be a problem during the summer. If possible, try to avoid folding it up because this can damage the electrical heating element within it. If you can, leave it lying flat on a spare bed or even between a mattress and a divan base. Better still, hang it up by its tapes, or else use a couple of trouser hangers, in a cool, dry cupboard. Always follow the manufacturer's care and servicing instructions.

It's time to replace your pillow if it flops over your arm!

KEEPING YOUR BATHROOM SPARKLING

Five minutes a day is all that's needed to restore order to a bathroom, especially if you get into the habit of cleaning up after yourself every time that you've used it. Giving your bathroom a thorough clean will be a lot easier if the bath has been rinsed out and if any soap and toothpaste splashes, stains and lime-scale deposits have not been allowed to build up. The following tips will help you to keep your bathroom sparkling.

A clean bathroom not only looks good, but it is essential to be hygienic.

- Once a week, give your bath a good clean, paying particular attention to any scummy tidemark and clogged-up plughole. Rubber plugs can be cleaned with turpentine.

- Before using it, make sure that any proprietary bath-cleaner is suitable for your type of bath. You'll require a non-abrasive cleaner if you have an acrylic, vitreous-enamel, cast-iron or steel bath.

- Glass-fibre baths and shower trays are best cleaned with a little washing-up liquid because even a mildly abrasive cleaner can wear through the outer layer of colour, leaving a patchy surface.

- Rust marks on baths can often be bleached out with a paste of cream of tartar or salt or lemon juice. (If you use lemon juice, you may have to keep adding more, however, and because it works slowly, you may need to leave it on for a day or so.) If any of these methods fail, and your bathtub is white tub, try rubbing a little hydrogen peroxide into the rust mark.

- Lime-scale deposits, which are common in hard-water areas, are most often found around taps. To remove lime scale from the spout of a tap, submerge it in a plastic bag or an empty yoghurt pot filled with lime-scale remover or white-wine vinegar.
- Be warned that a dripping tap will leave lime-scale deposits, and possibly even rust marks, on your bath. So stop the drip and change the washer!
- Chrome taps can be cleaned with a little household ammonia added to water, after which you should rinse the tap and polish it by drying it thoroughly. If you've no ammonia to hand, rubbing the tap with a damp cloth to which you've applied toothpaste will work just as well. Rub chrome taps with a mixture of salt and vinegar to remove any water deposits.
- The sealant between baths, basins and walls is hard to clean. Using a fungicide spray will halt any mould growth and will also discourage it from growing again.
- Clean shower screens with a solution of washing-up liquid and water, paying particular attention to any tracks, hinges and catches if the screen is a folding or sliding mechanism. Leave shower screens open – but shower curtains drawn – until they have dried to enable the air to circulate.
- After you've used them, hang non-slip shower and bath mats on a trouser hanger, which will enable both sides to dry thoroughly.

Clean taps with a dab of toothpaste on a damp cloth or even an old soft toothbrush which is ideal for getting at fiddly or hard to reach bits!

- Pep up washable shower curtains by adding 1/2 cup of white-wine vinegar to the rinsing water.
- Either descale a shower head with a proprietary cleaner or secure a plastic bag filled with white-wine vinegar around it. After that, use an old toothbrush to give the head a good scrub and thereby dislodge any stubborn deposits.
- A really clogged-up shower head needs unscrewing (make sure that you don't lose the rubber washer) so that you can soak it in a bowl of vinegar.
- If you live in a hard-water area, descale bathroom tiles and panels in showers by applying neat vinegar and leaving it on for ten minutes before rinsing it off.
- Smearing a paste made of bicarbonate of soda (baking soda) and household bleach onto the grout between tiles and leaving it to dry for an hour or two will clean the grout efficiently. Scrub off the paste using an old toothbrush and clean water.
- Possibly the most effective grout-cleaner is a proprietary oven-cleaning preparation. Spray it onto a small section of grout, wipe it off within two to three seconds and immediately rinse that section with water. Before doing so, make sure that you're wearing rubber gloves and that the room is very well ventilated.
- If you add a good splash of mouthwash to a bucket full of hot water and then mop a tiled bathroom floor with it, not only will the floor smell minty, but the solution will kill any bacteria.

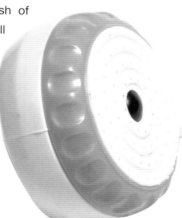

The very small holes in shower heads can become blocked with limescale. Clean heads by securing a plastic bag filled with white vinegar around it, and soaking well.

- Soak natural sea sponges in very salty water to prevent them from becoming slimy.

Don't discard an old, dried-up sponge, or one that has become slimy.

Soak in very salty water, then rinse.

A natural sponge, revived by its 'brine bath' and ready to use.

- Moisture on bathroom walls and ceilings can cause mould growth, so because oil repels water, wipe over these areas with a cloth to which you've applied a little baby oil once in a while.
- Although numerous products are available with which to clean lavatories, a daily routine of flushing, brushing and then flushing again will keep stains to a minimum. If you use a proprietary cleaner, remember never to mix it with bleach because the acid in the cleaner will react with the chlorine in the bleach to produce a toxic gas.

There are three more environmentally friendly lavatory cleaners than proprietary products (whose power lies in their mildly acidic agents): white-wine vinegar, which you should leave in the bowl for thirty minutes before flushing; two or three effervescent vitamin C tablets, which you should drop in the bowl and leave for a couple of hours; and, perhaps best of all, a cola drink (which can also remove rust from metal, while in an emergency, pouring a couple of cans of cola down the blocked plughole of a sink, shower or bath and leaving it for a couple of hours will often unblock it.)

The 'flush-brush-flush' routine will keep lavatory stains to a minimum.

- Don't regularly use bleach as a lavatory cleaner because it may cause the bowl's glaze to craze and crack, thus leading to the build-up of hard-to-shift stains. If your lavatory bowl is already crazed and cracked, be warned that it harbours germs and you should therefore consider replacing it.
- Unpleasant bathroom smells can be banished by striking a match – the flame will burn away those noxious gases!

Keep a lid on it: putting the toilet lid down before you flush – and keeping it down – stops bacteria from spreading.

CARING FOR YOUR KITCHEN

If they are to be safe and hygienic places, kitchens, like bathrooms, require daily cleaning. Clean worktops and surfaces with a damp cloth dipped in bicarbonate of soda (baking soda). Don't use harsh abrasives, however, because these will scratch the surfaces, enabling bacteria to grow undisturbed in the scratches, and also avoid using household cleaners that contain bleach because these may at least taint food and can be poisonous.

Cleanliness and order in the kitchen are vital to prevent illness and injury.

The following tips will help you to keep your kitchen shipshape, too.

- Be warned that laminates are not completely impervious to stains, including tea and coffee stains, which you can remove by mixing a paste of bicarbonate of soda (baking soda) and water, applying it to the mark and leaving it for fifteen minutes before rinsing it off.

Coffee – and tea – are probably the most common kitchen stain makers.

- Wooden surfaces need to be cleaned regularly, too, so wipe wooden food-preparation areas with a light antibacterial cleaner every two days or so.
- If you keep a plastic washing-up bowl that has wire wool embedded in the base in the sink, note that although the wire wool adds strength to the bowl, it may scratch the sink. It's therefore advisable to place a cloth in the sink and to rest the bowl on that.
- Clean a stainless-steel sink with a cloth soaked in warm, soapy water before rinsing the sink with hot water and then wiping it dry.

- Try removing any rust spots from a stainless-steel sink with a little neat washing-up liquid.
- Don't use silver-dip cutlery cleaners on stainless-steel draining boards because any splashes will cause a

Although tough and durable, stainless steel sinks do need special care.

rainbow effect that will eventually turn into a permanent dark stain.
- Avoid using bleach on stainless-steel surfaces because it can cause surface pitting.
- To remove any lime-scale deposits from a sink, particularly from around the plughole, rub the cut side of half a lemon over the surface.
- If you have a porcelain or 'Belfast' sink, note that an effective way of removing stains is to place a layer of paper towels on the bottom and around the base, to saturate the layer with bleach and then to leave it for five minutes before removing the paper and rinsing the sink clean.

Tap handles and tap heads also need to be kept clean.

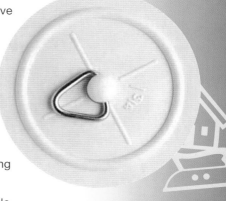

- Once a week, to keep the drain clean and dissolve any blockages that may have built up within it, place a cupful of washing soda over the plughole in your kitchen sink and pour a kettleful of boiling water over it.
- Don't pour grease or fat down the plughole in your kitchen sink because it will set like rock within the drain, thus blocking it. If you accidentally pour grease down the sink's plughole, pour boiling water down it immediately.
- If the rubber plug always comes out of the plughole when you're washing up, roughen its edges with a little steel wool.

Rubber plugs that slip out of plug holes should have their edges roughened with wire wool.

- If you have a waste-disposal unit in your sink, note that feeding the peel of citrus fruits into it will keep it smelling fragrant.

Cookers, grills and microwaves

Before cleaning any electrical appliance, make sure that the power is switched off (at the mains in the case of such hard-wired appliances as electric cookers and dishwashers, which are wired into fused connection units) and that portable appliances like kettles, toasters and food-processors have been unplugged from their sockets.

The cooker is the engine room of the kitchen. It needs to work safely and efficiently.

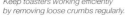

Keep toasters working efficiently by removing loose crumbs regularly.

The easiest way to keep a kitchen clean is to 'clean as you go' – wipe up spills as they happen.

You should give your cooker a wipe-over frequently, and in accordance with the manufacturer's instructions. (If you've lost the instruction booklet that came with your cooker, or a cooker that you've 'inherited' came without one, don't panic because it's possible to make a cooker clean and shiny without doing it any damage.) When you're cooking, it's also important to clean up after yourself as you go along because food that has dried or baked onto a hob will be hard to remove, so keep a damp sponge or cloth next to the cooker with which to wipe up any spills. If your cooker has an enamel surface, don't use any scourers or sharp or abrasive implements on it because once the surface has been scratched, it will have been damaged for good.

Most hobs can be washed down with a mixture of hot water and a general-purpose household detergent. For really stubborn spillages, however, as well as for any chrome or stainless-steel parts, mixing some bicarbonate of soda (baking soda) into a smooth paste with a little water, applying it to the spillage and leaving it on for ten to fifteen minutes before wiping it off with a soft cloth and then rinsing the area with a solution of white-wine vinegar and water can work wonders.

If you were smart enough to buy a self-cleaning oven, you won't have to bend, double yourself up or even hang upside down to clean it – just follow the manufacturer's instructions and don't use an oven-cleaner.

Although there are various cleaners on the market for those ovens that aren't self-cleaning, it's still important to follow the manufacturer's instructions. In addition, when applying the cleanser, make sure that you're wearing strong rubber gloves and also open the kitchen door if you can to ventilate the room.

A useful tip is to wipe a strong solution of bicarbonate of soda (baking soda) – 1 tablespoon of bicarbonate of soda to 250 ml (1/2 pint) of water – over a newly cleaned oven because you'll then find that the dirt comes off a lot easier when you clean it the next time. (You'll need to reapply the bicarbonate of soda after each oven-cleaning session.)

Coating a thick paste of bicarbonate of soda (baking soda) and water over the inside of a dirty oven window and leaving it on for ten to fifteen minutes before rinsing it off will clean away any ugly brown streaks, but remember only to do this when the glass is quite cool.

Food spillages in the oven tend to become baked on if they are left untreated, so as soon as you notice a spillage, sprinkle it with salt (which will absorb it) and then wipe off the salt when the oven is cool. If you want to banish the odour of burnt food at the same time, mix a little cinnamon into the salt (this works well for spills on the hob as well).

Indeed, it's a lot easier to prevent spillages from being baked

Cover spills in salt when they happen – it will absorb the spill and make it easier to remove.

onto ovens and grills than it is to clean them off later. A build-up of grease or fat in a grill tray can be dangerous, too, so line the tray with tinfoil with which to catch any spills. That way you can simply discard the tinfoil when it becomes dirty rather than having to wash the tray.

Drips from fat and oil can accumulate in grill pans and trays and can be dangerous. Line with foil and dispose of the grease regularly.

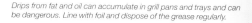

If you are fortunate enough to have a dishwasher, note that you can wash oven shelves in it, but however you wash them, make sure that they are dry before returning them to the oven in order to prevent them from rusting. Returning them to a warm oven will ensure that they become completely dry.

If you use a microwave oven, always place a lid – but not a metal one – over the cooking container to prevent messy splatters of food from coating the oven's walls and ceiling. Wiping out your microwave after each cooking session will also keep it clean.

A quick way of cleaning and deodorising your microwave is to fill a heat-resistant container with white-wine vinegar and to place it in the centre of the microwave before heating it on the microwave's highest setting for about one minute. Then don a pair of rubber gloves to protect your hands from the heat, remove the container and wipe the inside of the microwave with a soft cloth dipped in the hot vinegar.

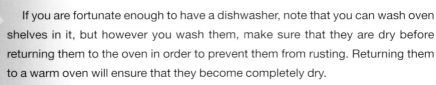

Alternatively, fill a heat-resistant bowl with water and add either a few drops of vanilla essence or three or four lemon slices, place the container in the centre of the microwave and heat it on high for thirty seconds.

If you find some hardened food deposits in your microwave, wet a dishcloth with water, place it in the middle of the microwave, set the microwave to high, 'cook' the wet cloth for about thirty seconds and the steam that is thereby created will help to loosen the hardened spillages. (Be careful when removing the cloth because it will be very hot.)

Microwave ovens are fast and efficient. Keep them that way by routine cleaning and maintenance.

Refrigerators and freezers

A fridge whose freezer compartment has a small glacier growing in it is inefficient and needs defrosting. To do this, remove any food (either store it in cool bags or ask a neighbour to keep it in his or her fridge-freezer for you for a day) and then turn off the power and unplug the fridge. Place a towel on the fridge floor to soak up the water that will be produced as the ice melts and put a tray on the floor to catch any drips. Leave the fridge door open while the ice melts. (You could use a hairdryer on a low setting to speed up the defrosting process, but if you do, remember to keep the heat away from any plastic parts.) While the freezer compartment is defrosting, take any removable trays, racks and shelves out of the fridge and give them a wash.

When the freezer compartment has defrosted, wash the inside of the fridge with a mixture of bicarbonate of soda (baking soda) and warm water; don't use any detergents – even washing-up liquid – because they can leave food-tainting odours. And if you wipe or brush a little glycerine over the inside of the freezer compartment after it has defrosted, the next time you defrost it, the ice will fall off in sheets, speeding up the whole process.

Speed up the defrosting process by playing the heat from a hairdryer over the ice.

Wipe up any food or drink spillages in fridges as soon as they occur, or you notice them, and note that wiping the inside of the fridge with a cloth moistened with a little white-wine vinegar once in a while will help to ward off mildew.

A simple, but effective, way of deodorising a fridge is to keep an open tub – or even an egg cup – filled with bicarbonate of soda (baking soda) on a fridge shelf, where it will absorb food odours for months. Really smelly fridges should be defrosted, cleaned and then left for a day or so with the door open and a bowl of clean cat litter positioned on the middle shelf.

If you are going away on holiday for a long period, it's advisable to clear your fridge of all foodstuffs before unplugging and defrosting it and then leaving it unplugged, with the door open, to await your return. If you don't do this, the likelihood is that you'll come home to a fridge full of evil-smelling green mould!

In general, freezers should be defrosted when the ice has built up to a thickness of 5 mm (1/4 inch), and if you usually keep your freezer tightly closed, it should only need defrosting once a year (choose a time when your food stocks are low – perhaps the New Year period, after all of the festive feasts have been eaten up). Before defrosting your freezer, remove any frozen foodstuffs and then either wrap them in several layers of newspaper and swaddle them in a blanket to prevent them from defrosting or ask a neighbour to store them in his or her freezer for you.

Now unplug the freezer and place two large pans of hot water inside it. Whatever you do, don't be tempted to pick off any of the ice with a sharp metal object because this may damage the freezer walls. Mop up the melting ice and water with a large towel, and when the freezer has completely defrosted, wipe the interior clean (you could also wipe some glycerine over the interior, which will aid the removal of ice the next time that you defrost the freezer). Switch the power back on and replace the foodstuffs before wiping down the exterior of the freezer with warm water.

To keep the exterior casings of white appliances sparkling, and also to prevent yellowing, wipe them with a solution made of 1/2 cup of household bleach, 1/2 cup of bicarbonate of soda (baking soda) and 8 cups of water and then rinse the exterior thoroughly.

Small electrical appliances

The most important thing to remember before cleaning any small electrical appliance is to switch off the power and unplug it, and also to avoid getting any of its electrical connections wet. When it comes to cleaning blenders and food-processors, check the manufacturer's instructions because although these have a number of parts that can be washed, some may not be suitable for dishwashers.

A kettle's innards tend to become 'furred up' with lime scale, and because an encrusted kettle takes longer to boil and uses more energy, it's advisable to keep it as scale-free as possible. To minimise the amount of scale that is deposited, the most important thing is not to leave water sitting in the kettle. A traditional way of reducing the amount of scale in a kettle is to place a small, rough seashell into it, which is said to attract the scale, thereby preventing it from being deposited over the inside of the kettle.

You can remove deposits that have already formed by pouring a solution consisting of equal parts vinegar and water into the kettle (don't fill the kettle more than half full

A seashell placed in a kettle. The limescale will attach itself to the shell, rather than the kettle.

because the vinegar will expand as it heats) and boiling it up. Leave the solution to become cold and then empty the kettle and rinse it out. Although this treatment will usually cope with a light deposit, to remove a heavy one you'll need to keep bringing the solution to the boil and rubbing the inside of the kettle as the solution cools (the vinegar will have softened the deposit, making it easier to remove).

Electric kettle elements soon become furred up with limescale. Boiled vinegar and water will help soften the scale away.

Doing the washing up

When it comes to washing up, the best advice is to do it straightaway because any food that is left on a plate will dry and harden, making removing it harder the later you leave it. If you can't wash dirty plates right away, leave them to soak instead.

There is a method to washing dishes by hand: glasses first – and one by one – then cutlery, then crockery and lastly pots and pans. Basically, because you're washing the less dirty pieces first, your washing-up water will stay cleaner for longer. Every item should be rinsed after it's been washed, and adding a dash of vinegar to your rinsing water will remove the alkalinity left by the soap and make most items shiny.

Sparkling china and glassware can be an attractive feature.

Here are some more useful washing-up tips.

- Rinse glasses that have contained milk or alcohol in cold water before washing them up.
- When placing glasses in the sink or bowl, take care to ensure that they don't chip or break and check that the water isn't too hot because this could shatter them.
- Before washing precious glasses or fine china, place a towel over the bottom of the sink or bowl to cushion them against its hard surface.
- Don't wash lead-crystal glassware in very hot water, and never in a dishwasher.
- If one glass becomes stuck inside another, fill the top glass with cold water, submerge the bottom glass in hot water and then gently pull away the top glass.

- The handle fixings of all but the most modern knives are vulnerable to heat and moisture, so if you're washing up old-style knives that have a resin, bone or ivory handle, avoid letting the bolster come into contact with the water when you're washing the blades.

- 'Stainless steel' is something of a misnomer because stainless-steel cutlery can, in fact, be stained by bleach and prolonged contact with acidic foods and drinks. Restore the shine to stainless-steel cutlery by rubbing it with an ordinary cork. If you're preparing for a special occasion, such as a dinner party, you could remove any fingermarks by rubbing stainless-steel cutlery with a soft cloth dipped in white-wine vinegar.

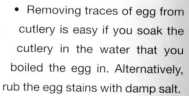

- Removing traces of egg from cutlery is easy if you soak the cutlery in the water that you boiled the egg in. Alternatively, rub the egg stains with damp salt.

- Remove tea stains from china by gently rubbing them with a soft cloth sprinkled with bicarbonate of soda (baking soda) or salt.

- China with a gold border needs special care: never put it into a dishwasher; wash it by hand in warm water; and don't rub detergent into the gold areas.

Cutlery – even after washing – often doesn't bear close scrutiny. A soft cloth dipped in white-wine vinegar will bring them up a treat.

DISHWASHER DOS AND DON'TS

If you're lucky enough to have a dishwasher, then do make sure that:

- any item that goes into it is dishwasher-safe (unlike wooden items, heat-sensitive plastics, cast iron and anodised aluminium, along with antique or handpainted china, which must all be washed by hand);
- you follow the manufacturer's advice regarding the type and amount of detergent that you should use. Too much detergent will make too many suds, thereby preventing the machine from cleaning its contents properly;
- you regularly check the inlet and outlet hoses for wear and tear and blockages;
- you regularly check that the filter is clean and that the spray arms aren't blocked;
- you occasionally run your dishwasher when it is empty, using a special interior-cleaner;
- you try out all of your dishwasher's cycles because you may well find that a shorter cycle cleans just as well as a longer one;
- you load dishes so that they are facing the direction of the spray and cups so that they are facing downwards.

DON'T:

- overload the baskets;
- wash precious glasses, china or items decorated with gold or metal strips in your dishwasher;
- mix stainless-steel cutlery with silver or silver-plated cutlery because the silver may become pitted and stained;
- run a dishwasher when it is only half full because this is a waste of both money and water. Instead, wait until you have a full load, and if necessary pre-rinse any items while they are waiting to be washed.

Pots and pans

Some simple strategies will keep your pots and pans sparkling clean.

- Soaking pots and pans after you've used them will make them easier to clean.

- Some non-stick surfaces simply require a wipe-over with a paper towel, but if a non-stick surface does become stained, mix 2 tablespoons of bicarbonate of soda (baking soda) with 1/2 cup of household bleach and 1 cup of water, transfer the mixture to

Shiny copper pans are too beautiful to be hidden away from sight.

the stained pan, heat it on the hob and let it boil for ten minutes (but don't let it boil over or boil dry). Then pour out the solution, wash the pan with soap and water, rinse it, dry it and finally rub a little vegetable oil over the surface.

- Food that has become caked onto baking trays, pots and pans can be dealt with in a very lazy way: just pour in some hot water, throw in a denture-cleaning tablet, leave it overnight and then wash the container the next morning.

Well maintained saucepans and lids should see you through years of service.

- Scorched pans can be saved! Remove as much of the burnt food as possible with a wooden or plastic utensil and then sprinkle the bottom of the pan with enough bicarbonate of soda (baking soda) to form a thick layer over the burnt area. Add some water, let the pan stand overnight and then scrape and lift off the burnt remains with a wooden or plastic utensil.
- Although aluminium pots and pans may become discoloured, they can be restored to their natural state by adding water and boiling an acidic food, such as lemon juice, apple peel or even an onion, in the pan.
- To prevent aluminium (and stainless-steel) pans from becoming discoloured and pitted in the first place, don't soak them or leave food in them for too long.
- Small rust marks on enamel pots and pans can be removed by rubbing them with a damp cloth sprinkled with a little bicarbonate of soda (baking soda).
- Cast-iron cookware must be kept completely dry to prevent it from rusting. Instead of washing the interior, try shaking salt over it and then wiping it clean. If you prefer to wash cast iron, however, remember to dry it thoroughly and then to rub a little oil lightly around the inside to keep it 'seasoned'. To clean the outside, either use a proprietary cleaner, such as an over-cleaner, or wipe it with a sheet of waxed paper while the pot is still hot.

Rubbing salt and vinegar, or salt and lemon juice, over a saucepan's copper bottom will restore its shine. It is worth noting, however, that the duller the copper, the better the heat-transference and thus the more efficient your saucepan!

Rusty baking tins can be revived by scouring them with half a raw potato and a sprinkling of powdered detergent. Pouring cola into the tray and leaving it overnight also does the trick.

- If a pot or pan continues to smell of something that was cooked in it, fill it with water, add a generous dash of vinegar and bring it to the boil, and the smell will vanish.
- Rusty baking tins can be revived by scouring them with half a raw potato and a sprinkling of powdered detergent. Pouring cola into the tray and leaving it overnight also does the trick.
- Woks are especially prone to rust, so emulate how the Chinese care for their woks by washing and drying the wok, then adding a drop of oil and heating it thoroughly. Finish off by rubbing the heated oil into the work with a clean paper towel, which will prevent it from rusting. Allow the wok to cool before storing it in a large plastic bag to protect it from gathering a layer of dust.

Kitchen odds and ends

Some kitchen items are often overlooked in the cleaning process, can-openers, mincers and grinders, thermos flasks and bread bins being just a few. Here are some final ideas for keeping your kitchen utensils clean, fresh and in good working order.

- Clean can-openers by feeding a piece of paper towel through their jaws.
- Remove debris from a mincer or grinder by running some bread or a raw potato through it before washing it.
- Keep bread bins mildew-free by wiping the inside with a little vinegar and then leaving the bread bin open to enable it to dry completely.

Feeding a paper towel through the jaws of a can opener removes any bits of grime lurking there.

Clean a badly stained vacuum flask by pouring in hot water, adding some uncooked rice, screwing on the lid and giving the flask a good shake before rinsing it with clean water.

- Leaving a piece of white blackboard chalk in a bread bin will absorb any moisture and keep the bread fresher for longer. (This tip is also a useful way of preventing silver from tarnishing in drawers.)
- Deodorise smelly vacuum flasks – and other types of closed jug – by rinsing them out with water to which you've added a little mustard. Alternatively, pour in a generous handful of salt, leave it for a day or so and then rinse out the flask with clean water.
- Before storing a vacuum flask, drop a lump of sugar into it to keep it fresh.
- Wooden chopping boards should be kept scrupulously clean (stains can be removed by scouring with a mixture of salt and lemon juice). Wash wooden chopping boards as soon as possible after use and never dry them flat, but instead stand them on one of their edges to enable both sides to dry at the same time, thereby preventing the board from warping.
- To get rid of any lingering food odours, such as onion, garlic or fish smells, as well as surface stains, on wooden chopping boards, rub them with the cut side of half a lemon dipped in salt.
- Remove any light stains and food odors from plastic chopping boards by rubbing them with the cut side of half a lemon.
- Before washing and drying rolling pins, sprinkle them with salt and rub it in with your hand to remove any loose particles of pastry.

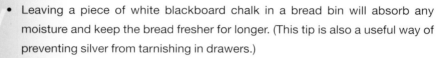

Clean up wooden chopping boards by rubbing with half a lemon.

KITCHEN AND FOOD TIPS

Most kitchens are the engine rooms of the home, and often also the centre of many different household activities. In addition, kitchens are frequently places where things can both go wrong and be wasted, not only food, but money, energy and time, too.

In the kitchen, it's important to get the basics right. It's no use being a brilliant cook, an ingenious menu-planner or a brilliant bargain-hunter if you don't take care to store foodstuffs properly. Food that has spoiled is food that has been wasted, while keeping food fresh means keeping it nutritious, safe and tasty. If you yearn for a freezer, but the reality is a fridge with a tiny freezer compartment, you can still keep fruit and vegetables, meat, fish and dairy products in perfect condition until you need them. Look after your fridge, too: defrost it frequently, wrap all foods to be stored within it and never put cooked foods into a fridge until they have been allowed to become completely cold.

In the following pages you'll find hints and tips on buying tinned foods and dry goods and on how to use them in rotation so that they don't end up sitting in your store cupboard beyond their 'use by' dates. If you do have a freezer, you'll also find information about blanching, freezing and thawing. Remember, however, that whatever types of foodstuff you store in your cupboards, larder, fridge or freezer, they must be as fresh as possible to begin with, so when you're shopping, check 'sell by' dates. If you're a keen bargain-hunter and are happy to buy reduced priced goods at the end of the day for immediate use, all well and good, as long as it is for immediate use.

When you're buying for storage purposes and find that something isn't in perfect condition when you unpack your shopping at home, take it back and complain! You're paying for quality and freshness, so make sure that you are getting what you're paying for!

The range of fresh produce available to us today means we can enjoy tasty, healthy food. Keeping it in first class condition is vital to preserve their goodness, and our health.

STOCKING UP: TOP TIPS FOR GROCERY SHOPPING

The following are useful tips to bear in mind when you're shopping for groceries.

- Don't go shopping for food when you're hungry! Not only will you buy too much, but you'll buy things that you want to eat there and then rather than items to store for later use.

- Make a shopping list! Otherwise you'll find yourself wandering around the supermarket aisles aimlessly and will end up buying items that you don't need.

- Get to know the workings of your local shops: find out when fresh foods are restocked, when the busy periods are and at what time of day bakery goods are reduced in price, for instance.

- Try before you buy: most delicatessen and grocers – and even big supermarkets – will let you taste-test 'loose' items like cheeses before buying them.

- If you don't see what you want on the shelf, ask for it because it may be in the back of the shop waiting to be shelved. If a local store doesn't have what you regularly need, ask the shopkeeper to order it for you – a shopkeeper's business is, after all, to serve you!

- Don't select food from a shop freezer that has been filled above its load line because the uppermost items may not be completely frozen as a result.

- Don't pack raw and cooked meats into the same shopping bag because the cooked meat could become contaminated by the raw meat's juices.

Special offers

If you're tempted to succumb to a special offer, remember that 'two for one' or 'three for two' price deals will only save you money if you regularly use the product

in question and have room to store the second or third item (even if you have really dirty hair, it'll take you a while before you use up that third bottle of shampoo!) Get round this problem by going shopping with friends and splitting the cost.

Similarly, coupons and vouchers can save you money, but only if you already use the product being promoted. Don't be tempted by the lure of vouchers and coupons for products that you don't usually buy because you could end up wasting your money.

Think before you buy and keep an eye on what your groceries cost.

Supermarket loyalty schemes can certainly save you money, so save your points and convert them into 'air miles' or use them to pay for Christmas or birthday festive dinners, for example. When shopping at the supermarket, also compare the prices of well-known brands and the supermarket's own brand to see which offers the best value for your money.

Bulk-buying

Buying in bulk is economical, but only if you have the space to store large quantities of items. Remember, too, that even dry goods, such as flour and cereals, as well as tinned foods, have expiry dates, so make sure that you'll be able to consume the food that you're buying in bulk before it passes its best.

Look carefully at supermarket shelves for special offers, and compare prices, weight for weight.

Bags or trays full of fresh fruit or vegetables may be a bargain, but they won't stay fresh for very long. Unless you can a) freeze them, b) you're a whiz at making jams and pickles or c) you're entertaining vegetarians very soon, you'll end up throwing away a great deal. Check that any raw meat that's being sold in bulk is suitable for home-freezing, too, and remember that you must never refreeze any previously thawed foodstuffs.

To save in the long term, bulk-buying means parting with a lot of cash upfront, so think carefully if you're on a tight budget. Don't assume that bulk-buying always means that items will be less expensive either, and keep a calculator handy so that you can work out unit prices for comparison.

Finally, don't forget that you've got to get your purchases home. Bulk-buying 48 tins of beans may cost you less, but if you don't have a car, how will you carry them all?

Take a calculator with you when you go shopping. You can work out unit prices quickly, and keep a running total on the cost of your goods.

E numbers: friends or foes?

A great deal is written and discussed about foodstuffs, not least their nutritional values and their effects on health. Much concern has recently been expressed about the incompatibility of 'healthy eating' and the use of artificial flavours, colours and additives, in particular, E numbers. Yet not all additives are synthetic – and some are, in fact, natural substances – so don't be surprised if you see a product labelled 'free from artificial additives' whose listed ingredients include E numbers. Becoming familiar with some of the most common E numbers, as listed below, will help you to decide whether a particular substance is a 'friend' or possible 'foe'.

E FRIENDS

- E100: also known as curcumin, this is an orange-yellow colouring that is extracted from turmeric root. It is mostly used to impart a 'sunshine' colour to 'red' cheeses and margarines, but is also used to colour biscuits.
- E300: this is simply vitamin C by another name. It's used to preserve certain foods and prevents fruit from turning brown and fatty foods from becoming rancid.
- E306: better known as vitamin E, this additive preserves fats and oils.
- E322: this soya extract, also known as lecithin, is used in low-fat spreads and as an emulsifier in many other products, including chocolate.

POSSIBLE E FOES

- E102: also known as tartrazine, this yellow dye is derived from coal tar and is used to colour smoked fish and soft drinks. It may cause headaches and has been linked with hyperactivity in children. It may also cause allergic symptoms, such as skin rashes, and can adversely affect asthmatics and people who are sensitive to aspirin.
- E220: sulphur dioxide, as it is also known, is usually used to preserve fruit (you'll find it listed on the ingredient labels of many packets of dried apricots, raisins, currants and other dried fruits). It is thought to provoke headaches and nausea and to aggravate the symptoms of asthma in some people.
- E320: this chemical preservative, also called butylated hydroxyanisole, is most commonly found in processed foods, drinks and snack products. Although it has been linked with hyperactivity in children, it is often found in the very foods and drinks that are aimed at them. People who suffer from asthma or allergies should avoid this additive, and no food containing it should be given to babies.

- E621: also known as monosodium glutamate, or MSG, this additive is used as a flavour-enhancer. Banned from baby foods, MSG can cause headaches, palpitations and dizziness in some people.

THE STORE CUPBOARD

A store cupboard should be dry, cool, closed and – it should go without saying – well stocked. Here are some tips to help you to maximise its efficiency.

- Write 'sell by' dates clearly on packets and tins.
- Rotate the stock in your cupboards (and fridge) so that the oldest purchases are used first and don't pass their 'best by' dates.
- Remember that once they've been opened, bottled foodstuffs will keep for only a limited period, and that some should be stored in the fridge. Make sure that you read their labels, which will give specific storage instructions.
- Note that once tinned foods have been opened, they should be treated as though they were fresh foods. If you don't use the entire contents of a tin, transfer the unused portion to a different container and store it in the fridge.
- Don't store herbs and pulses in glass jars because light will permeate the jar, destroying the herbs' colour and flavour and toughening the skins of pulses.
- It's best to store the contents of all opened packets in airtight containers, but if this isn't possible, you can keep the contents in their original packaging, as long as you've ensured that is undamaged and can be sealed.
- In common with ground spices, ground coffee soon loses its flavour and becomes bitter, so buy ready ground fresh coffee in small quantities and use it quickly. An economical alternative is to buy coffee beans and invest in a grinder, so that you can grind the beans as and when you need to.
- Regularly inspect tinned foods for signs of damage, discolouration or bulging and immediately discard any tins that have developed rusty seams, bulges or leaks.

Fruit and vegetables

Fresh fruit and vegetables are best bought in small quantities. Avoid storing fresh produce in the plastic packaging in which it may have been sold because air should circulate around fruit and vegetables to prevent them from sweating and becoming soggy.

Tips for storing fruit and vegetables

- Avocados: these fruits only begin to ripen when they are picked, a process that is slowed down when they are shipped in refrigerated conditions, which is why they're generally unripe and hard in shops. Keeping avocados cold will stop them from ripening, but to speed up the ripening process, store them in a warm place, such as an airing cupboard. Placing avocados in a plastic bag with a piece of banana peel, or burying them in a bowl of flour, also ripens them. A leftover avocado half can be prevented from ripening for a short while by leaving the stone in. Although you could alternatively squeeze a generous amount of lemon juice over the cut surface, this alters an avocado's flavour.

Apples: unblemished apples (remove any bruised or blemished ones to prevent them from contaminating the others with their rot) are best stored on a tray or rack. You can ripen apples – and pears – by placing them in a brown paper bag with an apple that is already ripe, punching a few ventilation holes into the bag and then storing the fruit in a cool, dark place for a couple of days.

- Melons: watermelons apart, when a melon is ripe, the end opposite the stalk should be slightly soft (you should be able to depress it gently with your thumbs) and the melon will also smell wonderful. When buying cantaloupes, look for ones that are evenly beige to grey in colour and avoid those that are hard and green because these will have been picked before they were fully ripe and won't be as sweet as those that were left a little longer (honeydew melons are the only melons that become sweeter after they have been harvested). Don't store melons in the fridge (unless you've placed them in an airtight container) because they will cause everything else in the fridge to taste and smell of melon. To identify a good watermelon, turn it over, tap it – it should sound firm – and look for tiny wormholes (don't worry: the worms can't penetrate the melon's tough skin, but wormholes are a sign that there's something very tasty inside!)

- Bananas: some people like their bananas hard, others like them soft and some even like them when they've turned a bit brown. Their skins will tell you how ripe bananas are: green tints mean that they aren't quite ripe, but will be ready for eating after spending a day in a warm place; brown spots indicate that they are starting to ripen, and the more spots, the riper – and softer. Don't discard really ripe bananas because they're delicious when whizzed with yoghurt in a blender.

Garlic: although garlic cloves and bulbs are best stored in a cool, dry place, a useful time-saving tip is to peel off the skins and to place the cloves in a small jar of olive oil. Not only will this extend the garlic's life, but you'll also end up with some garlic-flavoured oil.

Note that if you store bananas in the fridge, you'll prevent them from ripening, but the cold will darken their skins. A final tip is that bananas always seem to last longer when they're in a bunch!

- Grapes: grapes never last long, if only because every time people pass a bunch, they pull off a couple! You can, however, preserve a bunch of grapes for quite some time – several months, in fact – by selecting a bunch that has a good length of stalk, pushing the stalk into a bottle or jar filled with cold water and a little charcoal and then keeping the grapes in a cool place until you need them.

- Lettuce: lettuce is the one exception to the no-plastic rule because it seems to thrive if it is loosely wrapped in a large plastic bag and kept in the fridge. A good way of reviving a limp lettuce is to slice off a sliver of the stem end and place the remaining lettuce in a bowl of cold water (to which some people add a dash of lemon juice). Individual leaves can be revived if you sprinkle them with cold water, wrap them in a teatowel and pop them in the fridge for an hour or so.

- Carrots (and beetroots and turnips): cut off any green, leafy tops because these will otherwise continue to draw nutrients from the roots. Like all root vegetables, carrots will last longer if they are kept in a cold, dry, dark place, with good ventilation.

After you've cut a lemon in half, place the halves cut side down on a saucer, cover them with an inverted glass and store them in a cool place.

- Lemons: whole lemons will keep for weeks if you store them in egg cartons in the fridge, and it also seems that the less air that circulates around a lemon, the longer it will keep. After you've cut a lemon in half, place the halves cut side down on a saucer, cover them with an inverted glass and store them in a cool place. If you need only a small amount of lemon juice, try piercing a whole lemon with a wooden cocktail or kebab stick, squeezing out however much juice you need and then plugging the hole with the stick – by excluding air in this way, you'll be able to continue storing the lemon for some time.

- Celery: celery starts to lose its flavour as soon as it is washed, so if it's really flavourful celery that you're after, buy the dirtiest bunch you can and don't wash it until you need it. (Most supermarkets, however, sell squeaky clean celery minus its leafy tops, which is a shame because these parts have the strongest flavour and taste wonderful when finely chopped and cooked with rice.) The best way to store a piece of celery is to stand the stalk upright in a glass of water before placing it in the fridge.

- Parsley: there always seems to be enough parsley in a shop-bought bunch to garnish a state banquet, let alone a single meal! Parsley is wasted once it starts to turn yellow, and a good way of keeping it at its best is to finely chop a bunch, roll the chopped parsley into lots of small balls, lay them on a piece of paper towel or foil and then to pop them into the fridge's ice compartment or the freezer. When each ball has frozen, transfer them to a plastic bag and return them to the ice compartment or freezer. Every time that you need a little chopped parsley, just defrost a ball! Fresh parsley is probably the finest breath-

freshener known to humankind,so if you've overdone the garlic, chew some parsley!

- Herbs: although you can buy ready prepared herbs, be they dried or freeze-dried and preserved in jars, nothing beats the aroma and flavour of home-grown herbs. Most supermarkets now sell 'growing herbs', which are remarkably tolerant plants in pots that will readily grow on a windowsill in the kitchen, enabling you to pull off a leaf or two as and when you need them. A further advantage is that growing basil in a pot like this will help to keep flies out of the kitchen; rosemary will deter weevils; mint will ward off ants; and sage and thyme will keep moths at bay! If you rub a sage leaf over your teeth and gums after brushing your teeth at night, not only will it freshen your breath, but it will battle gum disease, too (indeed, sage has long been used in toothpaste). Steeping a few sage leaves in boiling water for a couple of minutes and letting the tea cool before drinking it is also an effective cure for indigestion.

Mushrooms: store mushrooms in a cool, dark place, but not the fridge. I find that they last longer if they are wiped dry and laid on a piece of paper kitchen towel. If you're after really neatly, evenly sliced mushrooms, take an egg-slicer to them!

- Onions: onions are easy to store – just put them into a vegetable basket or wire rack. The trick to preventing them from rotting is to keep the bulbs apart so that air can circulate around them. If you fancy hanging a plait of onions, like those seen in France, in your kitchen, but the shop-bought ones no longer have the necessary long, green leaves, improvise by using a pair of old nylon tights (with lots of ladders in them to enable the air to get in). To do this, drop an onion into each 'foot', tie a knot in the 'leg' immediately above it and then add more onions and knots until the legs have been filled. (If you want, you could twist the legs around each other so that the effect is less like a pair of old tights stuffed with onions.) Every time you need an onion, just cut one off from the bottom of a leg. (This is also a good way to store bulbs that you've lifted from the garden.)

- Mushrooms: store mushrooms in a cool, dark place, but not the fridge. I find that they last longer if they are wiped dry and laid on a piece of paper kitchen towel. If you're after really neatly, evenly sliced mushrooms, take an egg-slicer to them!

- Olives: the cheapest way of buying olives – and of getting the best selection – is to buy them loose. Then label and date a jar, transfer the olives to it and pour over enough olive oil (they will naturally keep well in their own 'juice') to cover them. Although olive oil lasts for only one year – which is why you should label the jar – you can keep topping up the jar with olives and oil for about nine months. After that, use up the oil when cooking.

Peas: to store peas, wash them in cold water – but don't dry them – place them in a perforated plastic bag and then pop the bag into the fridge.

- Potatoes: stop potatoes from sprouting by storing them in a cool, dry place with a few apples. If you've peeled too many – or have peeled them in preparation for cooking – put the peeled potatoes in a bowl, cover them with water and place the bowl in the fridge.

Once a potato has begun to sprout, it's no good for eating.

- Tomatoes: some people like their tomatoes rock hard, while others prefer them soft. Green tomatoes, along with any that haven't fully ripened, are best stored in a dark place (exposing them to sunlight simply makes them soft, not ripe). To ripen them, place them either in a brown paper bag with an apple or in a drawer, stalk side up, and leave them until they've turned rosy red.

THE REFRIGERATOR

The temperature inside your fridge should be between 0°C (32°F) and 5°C (41°F). If your fridge does not have a thermometer, buy one because this will tell you whether your fridge is running at the right temperature. If it is too warm, food won't be chilled correctly and bacteria will start to multiply, while if it is too cold, ice particles will form within the food. Knowing your fridge's inside temperature means that you will be able to adjust it, perhaps turning it down to a lower setting in winter, or switching it to a higher setting in summer.

Sunlight makes tomatoes soft, but not ripe. To ripen tomatoes, store them with an apple in a paper bag.

IN ORDER TO KEEP YOUR FOOD IN PERFECT CONDITION, FOLLOW THESE OTHER SIMPLE GUIDELINES, TOO.

- Defrost the ice compartment, if it has one, and clean your fridge regularly.
- Don't leave the fridge door open! The fridge will use less energy if you keep the door shut because every time that it is opened the temperature rises within and the fridge then has to work to lower it again.
- Don't overload your fridge with food because the cold air should be able to circulate freely.
- Remember that any food that goes into the fridge must be completely cool, so never place warm food inside it. If you're in a hurry, transfer the warm food to a wide container, place it in a sink of cold water and stir the food frequently to speed up the cooling process.
- Never store raw and cooked meats together, but instead ensure that they are wrapped and stacked separately.
- Always store cooked foods on shelves above raw foods to avoid any juices dripping down from the raw foods onto the cooked ones and contaminating them.
- Surface moisture is an ideal breeding ground for bacteria, so always remove any packaging from fresh meat, poultry or fish, pat the flesh dry with a paper kitchen towel and then place each piece either into a separate, closed container or on a plate that you should then cover loosely with tinfoil or a bowl. Doing this will also enable air to circulate freely around the produce.
- Make sure that you wrap up any strong-smelling foods to prevent the other foods – especially eggs – in your fridge from taking on their flavour. Sliced or cut onions, lemons and garlic will all impart their flavour, as will melon portions.

Store eggs with the pointed end facing downwards. If you keep them on the specially designed egg shelf in the fridge door, your eggs will keep for up to ten days. And if you store them in their box or in a bowl in the lowest part of the fridge, they'll remain fresh for up to three weeks.

- Note that food that has been chilled in a fridge won't taste as flavourful as room-temperature food, so before serving it, remove food from the fridge and leave it to warm up to room temperature.

Freezers and ice-box compartments

The inside temperature of your freezer should be between -18°C (0°F) and -23°C (-10°F). Rather than relying on the freezer gauge, which may not always be completely accurate, check your freezer's temperature with a specialised freezer thermometer.

UNDERSTANDING THE STAR RATINGS

- Freezers and refrigerators that have an ice-box compartment are now marked with a star rating that tells you how long food can be safely stored, as follows:
- a one-star (*) freezer or ice-box compartment will store ready frozen foods safely for one week;
- a two-star (**) freezer or ice-box compartment will store ready frozen foods for up to one month;
- a three-star (***) freezer or ice-box compartment will store ready frozen foods for up to three months;
- a four-star (****) freezer is the only freezer that is suitable for freezing fresh foods and for storing it for up to 3 months

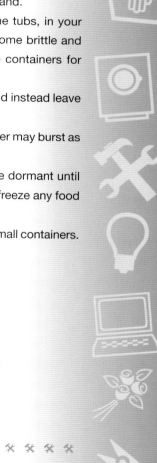

Freezer dos and don'ts

To freeze food safely, observe the following guidelines.

- Wrap all food destined for the freezer and seal it in an airtight container. Plastic containers with snap-on lids are best for liquids and brittle items, while freezer-weight plastic bags and twist-ties or tape are suitable for other produce.
- Don't put acidic foods (such as tomato-based pasta sauces) into foil freezer dishes because the acidity may eat holes in the foil.
- Place foil-wrapped foods in plastic freezer bags.
- Don't freeze glass jars in case they crack as their contents expand.
- If you want to use plastic food containers, such as margarine tubs, in your freezer, freeze the container first because some plastics become brittle and split at low temperatures and may therefore not be suitable containers for frozen foods.
- When freezing liquids, don't fill the container right to the top and instead leave at least 2.5 cm (1 inch) of space to allow for expansion.
- Don't freeze bottled or canned fizzy drinks because the container may burst as the contents expand.
- Because low temperatures won't kill bacteria (which simply lie dormant until the food is defrosted, when they start to multiply again), don't freeze any food that isn't absolutely fresh.
- To speed up both freezing and defrosting times, freeze food in small containers.
- Label and date containers so that you know what they contain and when the contents should be consumed.
- Never refreeze defrosted food. Food can be cooked and then frozen, however.

Make sure that containers for use in freezers are made of suitable materials and have airtight, close-fitting lids.

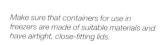

What freezes well and what doesn't

Some types of food will freeze extremely well, as long as you observe the following guidelines.

- Only freeze fish that is absolutely fresh. Scale and gut smaller round fish and freeze them whole; when preparing larger round fish, also remove their heads and tails. Flat fish should be cut into fillets, and each fillet should be separated from the others prior to being frozen by being laid between sheets of waxed paper. Fish can be kept frozen for up to six months.

- Separate cutlets, chops, steaks and burgers from one another with waxed paper and wrap all types of meat in several layers of packaging to protect them from freezer-burn. Because slow freezing diminishes its flavour, freeze fresh meat quickly. Pork will keep in the freezer for up to nine months, beef and lamb for up to a year.

- Before freezing poultry (or game birds), remove the giblets, which should be frozen separately. Do not stuff poultry before freezing it because this will lengthen both the freezing and thawing times. All fresh birds must be washed and dried thoroughly before being frozen. Poultry and game will keep for up to nine months in the freezer, but giblets should not be stored for longer than six months.

- Vegetables must be blanched before being frozen to destroy the enzymes that cause discolouration and loss of flavour. To do this, dip the vegetables in boiling water for two to five minutes, depending on their thickness, and then cool them by placing them under running cold water.

- Although frozen fruit retains its flavour, it can lose some of its texture when it is thawed. Only freeze fruits that are ripe, but still firm; overly soft fruit is best puréed before being frozen. Freeze whole soft fruits, such as berries, by laying them on paper-lined trays in the freezer. After each berry has been individually frozen, transfer them to a single plastic freezer bag or container and return them to the freezer.

SOME TYPES OF FOOD DON'T FARE THAT WELL WHEN FROZEN, HOWEVER, AS SUMMARISED BELOW.

- When frozen, uncooked eggs in their shells will burst, while hard-boiled eggs will become rubbery.
- When frozen mayonnaise is thawed, it will curdle and its ingredients will separate.
- During the thawing process, the components of frozen single cream and yoghurt (but not double or whipping cream) will separate.
- Frozen jelly will become runny when it is thawed, as will all dishes made with gelatine, as well as those that include single cream and egg yolks.
- The freezing process makes whole cooked potatoes (but not mashed potatoes) rather tough.
- Foods that have a high moisture content don't freeze well, so don't freeze lettuce, raw tomatoes, cucumbers, watercress or celery unless you like them limp and mushy.
- If frozen, avocados, aubergines and bananas will become discoloured and will lose their texture.
- Dishes that include garlic can taste odd (rather musty) when frozen and then thawed, so if such a dish is destined for the freezer – even if it's for a very short time – leave out the garlic before freezing it and instead add it after the dish has been defrosted.

Some foodstuffs, like aubergines, lose their texture if frozen raw. It's better to cook them first in a recipe, then freeze the whole dish.

Dos and don't when thawing frozen foods

Whether you've bought a ready frozen product or have removed an item from your freezer, it's important to follow these simple thawing rules to ensure that the food will be safe to eat.

- Do let frozen meat thaw out slowly in a fridge or cool place. Once it starts to defrost, the dormant bacteria within the meat will become active and multiply, and if they are in a warm place, they will multiply more quickly.
- Remove the wrapping from frozen poultry and place the bird in a bowl to catch the liquids that are released during the thawing process. Never run hot or warm water over poultry to speed up the thawing rate, and make sure that the bird has thawed completely before washing out and drying it in preparation for cooking it.
- Cook frozen foods as soon as they have thawed completely.
- Unless it has since been cooked, never refreeze uncooked food after it has been thawed and never refreeze cooked foods that have been thawed once already. The rule for fresh foods is: freeze, thaw and cook; the rule for cooked or prepared dishes is: freeze, thaw, reheat thoroughly.

FOOD-HYGIENE TIPS

Although we often worry about food poisoning when we eat in restaurants or order food from take-away outlets, we are more likely to become sick as a result of our own lapses in hygiene. It's vital to observe the following basic food-hygiene measures.

- Wash your hands before and after preparing raw meat, poultry and fish.

Don't transfer bacteria from one board to another. Use one chopping board for raw meats and fish, another for cooked foods.

- Don't use the same chopping board when cutting up raw and cooked meat.
- Bring food to the boil quickly and cook it thoroughly.
- Don't keep food warm for long periods, but instead eat it as soon as possible after it's been cooked.

Be extra careful when preparing and cooking poultry and rolled joints of meat. Rolling the outside of the meat to the middle will carry bacteria from the outside to the centre, and if the cooking temperature in the middle of the joint is not hot enough, the bacteria will multiply. To cook it safely, the centre of the meat must be at least 17.2°C (63°F) for twenty minutes, but in order for food to reach this temperature, your oven must be far hotter. Although there are lots of ways of telling whether a joint or a chicken is 'done', by far the most accurate is to insert a specialised thermometer into the centre of the meat when it comes out of the oven.

Rolled joints of meat need high oven temperatures so the centre of the joint is cooked properly.

FINALLY, DON'T WAIT SO LONG BEFORE EATING IT THAT YOUR FOOD GROWS ITS OWN 'FUR COAT' OR APPEARS TO MOVE OF ITS OWN ACCORD! IMMEDIATELY DISPOSE OF ANY FOOD THAT:

- smells 'off' or unusual;
- is slimy in moist areas;
- is discoloured;
- has unusual white or coloured patches or spots;
- has become infested with insects;
- has passed its 'use by' date;
- you know you'll never eat and is just taking up space in your cupboard!

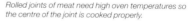

OVEN TEMPERATURES

	°F	°C	gas mark
Very cool	225–250	110–130	1/4–1/2
Cool	275–300	140–150	1–2
Moderate	325–350	170–180	3–4
Moderately hot	375–400	190–200	5–6
Hot	425–450	220–230	7–8
Very hot	475	240	9

CHEF'S TIPS

The following tips will give you a helping hand in the kitchen.

Ways with vegetables

Here are some top tips for serving the perfect vegetables.

- Soaking dried beans, peas and other legumes overnight in water to which a teaspoon of bicarbonate of soda (baking soda) has been added is the traditional way of helping them to retain their colour, also making them softer, thereby cutting down the cooking time. Some of their vitamin C content will, however, be lost.

Soaking dried beans overnight in water will cut down on cooking times the following day.

- Adding salt to dried peas and beans at the beginning of the cooking process will cause them to become as hard as bullets, so add salt at the end instead.

- Fresh peas in the pod don't need to be shelled before cooking and, indeed, retain more of their flavour if cooked in their pods. When they are ready, the pods will open and float to the surface of the water, making them easy to remove.

- Adding a little milk to a cauliflower's cooking water will keep the florets white.

The smell of a cabbage or cauliflower being cooked can be reduced by placing a piece of bread on top of it. Other ways of lessening a cabbage or cauliflower's cooking odour are to add a whole walnut or stalk of celery to the boiling cooking water.

- A single helping of broccoli will provide you with three times your daily vitamin C requirement; before cooking broccoli, make an 'X'-shaped incision at the base of each stalk to help it to cook as quickly as the florets.
- Small sprouts are both tastier and less wind-inducing than larger ones!
- Cook two different types of vegetable at the same time without affecting the flavour of either by wrapping them in kitchen foil before placing them in the cooking water.
- Eliminate the lingering odour of garlic on your hands by rubbing them with coffee grounds. Likewise, garlicky breath can be 'cured' by chewing a coffee bean.

Inserting a matchstick between a saucepan and its lid will let out just enough steam to prevent the water from boiling over.

- Make your own garlic salt by crushing a clove of garlic on a chopping board that has been liberally sprinkled with salt. Store your garlic salt in an airtight jar.
- To chop onions without shedding tears, chill them in the fridge for an hour or so before slicing them (the lower temperature slows down the speed with which the tear-inducing liquid within onions evaporates). Because tearing, rather than cleanly slicing, an onion releases more of the culprit liquid, it also helps to use a very sharp knife. If onions cause your eyes to stream, peel them under running water. Some people also advocate holding a fork or spoon between your clenched teeth; others advise cutting the bottom, root end of the onion before the top; still more maintain that a lighting candle in the kitchen solves the problem.
- Some people say that you can remove the lingering odour of onions from your fingers by placing all five on the handle of a stainless-steel spoon and running cold water over your hand. To banish a really persistent odour, try covering your hands with underarm deodorant (but rinse it off after a couple of minutes).
- When a recipe calls for fried onions and garlic, fry the onion first, and when it is hot, add the garlic, which burns easily and requires less cooking time.
- Sauté mushrooms over a high heat to keep them tender.
- To remove tomato skins, place the tomatoes in a bowl, pour boiling water over them, leave them for a minute or two and then immerse them in cold water. This should cause the skins to split, enabling you to peel them off easily.

Remove a pepper's skin by skewering the pepper and holding it over a naked flame until the skin has become charred all over. Rub off the charred skin with a piece of paper kitchen towel.

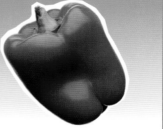

- Stuffed peppers will keep their bright colour if you coat them with olive oil before baking them.
- Standing stuffed peppers – and tomatoes – in a muffin tray before baking them will help them to maintain their shape.
- Reduce the amount of time that it takes to bake potatoes by sticking a small metal skewer (a large, clean, galvanised nail will work just as well if you don't have any skewers) through the middle to conduct the heat. Alternatively, boil the potatoes in their skins for ten to fifteen minutes before finishing them off in a hot oven.

The most versatile vegetable: baked, boiled, mashed or chipped – tasty potatoes are irresistible.

- Left-over baked potatoes? To bake them again, dip them in water and cook them in a preheated oven at 150°C (300°F). Alternatively, scoop out the cold flesh and either grate it or chop it into small pieces. Season the potato flesh, shape it into potato cakes, then sprinkle over a little paprika and fry until hot and crispy.
- Roast potatoes will be crisper if you sprinkle them with a little seasoned flour halfway through their roasting time. To speed up the roasting process, boil the potatoes until they are almost done, drain off the water, shake them in a colander so that the outsides become 'fluffy' and then roast them until they are crisp.
- Make mashed potatoes lighter and fluffier by adding heated milk to them before mashing them.
- Soggy mashed potatoes? This is probably because the potatoes were cooked a little too long. Make them fluffy by stirring in some powdered milk.

Ways with bread, rice and pasta

Cooking carbohydrates is easy if you follow these clever tips.

- Covering rising bread dough with a lightly greased piece of plastic – even a plastic carrier bag – will keep in the warmth and encourage the dough to rise faster without forming a crust.
- Give home-made bread a crusty finish by brushing it with a little salty water halfway through the baking time, when the top has become firm.
- Bread will shrink less during the baking process if you place a tin of water on the floor of the oven.
- It's said that keeping a large, washed and dried potato in the bread bin keeps bread fresh for longer.
- Turn stale bread into breadcrumbs either by breaking up the crusts in a blender or by drying out some slices in a preheated oven at 150°C (300°F) for ten minutes, then breaking them into pieces, putting the pieces into a bag and crushing them with a rolling pin.
- The correct way to serve caviar is on cold toast. Put the fish eggs on hot toast, and they'll melt and become runny.
- Adding a few drops of lemon juice to the cooking water will keep rice white.

- Rescue rice that has stuck to the bottom of the pan and burnt by tipping it into a clean saucepan and placing a crust of fresh bread over the top, which should get rid of the burnt taste. If you have burnt the rice before it has finished cooking, transfer it to a clean saucepan, add some more water and then the bread crust.
- To make rice more special, reconstitute a packet of dried vegetable-soup mix according to the instructions and add it to the cooking water. Not only will this 'stock' season the rice, but it will also add colour – and vegetables!
- Adding a teaspoonful of oil or a small knob of butter to pasta's salted cooking water will both prevent the pasta pieces from sticking together and stop the water from boiling over. For those who prefer a low-fat alternative, when the pasta has just cooked, add 15 ml (a tablespoonful) of cold water to the pan before draining it.

Home-made pasta is fiddly to make, while fresh pasta (which is also more yellow in colour) is more expensive than dried pasta. Impress your guests by cheating and adding two drops of yellow food-colouring to dried pasta's cooking water.

Ways with soups and stews

These ingenious ideas will help you to serve up delicious soups and stews.

- Make a thin soup thicker and creamier by adding some instant-potato powder.
- Adding salt to soups and stews early in the cooking process will enhance their flavour.
- Rescue overly salty soup by adding either a little sugar or some grated carrots. If it's still too salty, throw in a whole, peeled, raw potato, bring the soup to the boil and then remove the potato, which will have absorbed much of the salt.
- If a recipe specifies fresh herbs, but you only have dried, halve the amount indicated in the recipe.
- Adding a dash of sherry (the correct drink to accompany soup courses) will enliven even the blandest of tinned soups.
- Don't throw away left-over wine, but instead pour it into an ice-cube tray, freeze it and then drop the wine cubes into soups and stews to add flavour.
- Too much garlic? Throw in some parsley! Too spicy? Add some plain yoghurt!
- Remove excess fat from casseroles and stews by first allowing the dish to cool and

Where a recipe calls for herbs, you can use half the stated quantity of dried herbs in place of fresh.

the fat to settle on the surface and then lifting out the excess with a cold spoon and blotting up any remnants with kitchen paper. Brushing a lettuce leaf over the surface of the dish also works well, as does straining off the liquid and dropping in a few ice cubes; after the grease has congealed around them, lift them out with a slotted spoon.

- Dropping a child's large, clean marble into a slow-cooking sauce or stew after it has thickened will stir the sauce and prevent it from sticking and burning.
- Adding 15 ml (a tablespoon) of vinegar to a beef stew or curry at the start of the cooking process will both add flavour and tenderise even the toughest meat, while adding some left-over beer will give stews and casseroles a rich colour and flavour.
- When reheating stews and casseroles, bring them slowly to the boil and cook them at that heat for at least ten minutes to ensure that no bacteria survive.

Ways with spices, sauces and condiments

Add piquancy to dishes by following these ways with spices, sauces and condiments.

- Make your own instant seasoning by mixing 6 parts salt to 1 part black pepper.
- On a low-salt or salt-free diet? Garlic and onion powder, oregano, basil and white pepper all make healthy, but tasty, alternatives.
- Adding a few grains of rice to a salt shaker will ensure that the salt comes out freely.
- Mixing it with water gives English mustard powder a strong flavour; mixing it with milk results in a milder flavour; while mixing it with beer imparts a spicy tang. (A former Desert Rat informs me that a couple of tins of mustard powder can be used in an emergency to seal cracks in car – or tank! – radiators.)

White pepper won't clog in its pot or shaker if you add a dried pea.

- When making curries, frying the spices in a little oil first, rather than adding them to the other ingredients in powder form, will both remove their 'raw' flavor and make them easier to digest. Fry spices quickly over a medium heat, keeping a constant eye on them because they burn easily.

- Left-over wine can be added to white-wine vinegar to make your own, unique wine vinegar, although you'll need to experiment with quantities to suit your taste.

- Olive oil that has solidified in its bottle because it has become too cold can be made liquid again by standing the bottle in a jug of warm water. (Olive oil's flavour is unaffected by changes in temperature, however.)

- Lumpy sauces? Smooth them out by whisking them really hard in the saucepan. Alternatively, rub them through a fine sieve or purée them in a blender. In an emergency, you could even pour the sauce into a bottle, screw on the lid and shake the bottle like a cocktail!

- If your home-made mayonnaise separates, rescue it by beating in an extra egg yolk a little at a time.

- Make your own sour cream by adding 15 ml (a tablespoon) of lemon juice to 300 ml (1/2 pint) of fresh cream.

- Make your own allspice by mixing 1 1/2 teaspoons of ground cloves with 1 1/2 teaspoons of ground cinnamon.

A vigorous whisking can smooth out lumpy sauces and rescue homemade mayonnaise.

Ways with eggs

Eggs are among the most versatile of foods, and these tips will make them even more so.

- Test eggs for freshness by placing them in a deep bowl of cold water. If they rise to the surface, throw them away (air permeates stale eggs and makes them lighter). If they tip to one side, use them quickly. If they lie on their sides, however, you'll know that they're fresh.
- Don't put all of your eggs in one basket, that is, unless you mark the older eggs – those that should be used first – with an 'X'.
- Separate the white from the yolk of an egg by cracking the egg into a saucer and placing a small glass over the yolk. Then hold the glass and saucer firmly together, tilt the saucer and pour the white into your mixing bowl.
- Egg whites whip better when they are placed in a large glass or metal bowl and are at room temperature. Note that any trace of yolk will make them difficult to beat, however, and that adding a pinch of salt will ensure a dry, fluffy result. When making meringues, rub the inside of your mixing bowl with the cut side of half a lemon to remove any trace of grease.

Eggs that float should be discarded because air has got in. A really fresh egg will lie on its side in a bowl of water.

- If you find a bit of yolk in an egg white, holding a small, clean cloth that you've soaked in hot water and then wrung out near the yolk will act like a magnet and draw the yolk from the egg white.
- If you rinse the mixing bowl with water before beating egg yolks, you'll find that the yolks slide out easily rather than sticking to the sides of the bowl.
- If you find yourself with left-over egg yolks, drop them into a bowl of water, store it in a cool place and they'll keep for several days.
- Left-over egg whites will keep in the fridge for up to seven days if you cover them with clingfilm.
- Eggs should be at room temperature before they're cooked, so remove them from the fridge or a cool storage area about thirty minutes before you plan to use them.
- Don't place cold eggs in hot water because they'll crack. Instead, place them in cold or lukewarm water and bring it to the boil.

Piercing the end of an egg with a pin before boiling it will stop it from cracking. If an uncooked egg is already cracked, however, adding some vinegar to the cooking water will seal it.

- Plunging hard-boiled eggs into cold water as soon as they're cooked will prevent a black ring from forming around the yolks.

- If you prefer the yolks of your hard-boiled eggs to be dead centre, stir the eggs gently, but continuously, with a wooden spoon while you're cooking them to prevent the yolks from settling on one side.

- To cut hard-boiled eggs 'cleanly', dip your knife into boiling water.

- Scrambled eggs and omelettes generally taste better in restaurants than at home because chefs add a dash of sherry. Test this trade secret for yourself!

- It's not impossible to enjoy a fat-free fried egg. Place a heat-proof dish over a pan of boiling water and when the plate has become really hot, crack an egg onto it and let it cook.

- Don't wash bowls or implements that have been used for beating eggs in overly hot water because this will 'bake' on the traces of egg, making them harder to remove.

- Remember that egg yolk tarnishes silver, so don't let your finest cutlery come into contact with it.

Dried-on egg on cutlery can be tough to remove, so rinse off any egg first in cold water, so it's not baked on.

Ways with dairy produce

Make dairy produce go further with the help of these useful hints.

- Milk that's just about to 'turn' can be restored to freshness by adding a pinch of bicarbonate of soda (baking soda) to it. If it's too far gone, however, remember that sour milk can be wonderful when used for baking light scones and cakes. If, on the other hand, a recipe calls for sour milk and you don't have any, simply add a little lemon juice, or even vinegar, to milk to sour it.

The daily pint of milk's freshness can be maintained by careful storage.

- Before heating milk in it, rinse a saucepan in water to prevent the milk from sticking to the sides.

- If, when you are heating it, milk threatens to boil over the rim of the saucepan, quickly take the saucepan off the heat and give it a short, sharp knock.

- If milk tastes burnt after you've heated it, banish the scorched taste by adding a pinch of salt.

- Note that whipped cream will go further – and will also be less fattening – if you whip it with plain yoghurt.

- You'll find whipping cream easier if the bowl and utensils are cold.

- If cream won't whip up properly, try stiffening it by adding a drop or two of lemon juice.

- If you fold an egg white into whipped cream that has become watery, chill it thoroughly and then beat it again, the cream should fluff up nicely.

✷ ✷ ✷ ✷ ✷ ✷ ✷ ✷ ✷ ✷ ✷ ✷ ✷ ✷ ✷ ✷ ✷ ✷ ✷ ✷

- Cheese tastes best when it's not too cold, so store it in a cool larder rather than a fridge.
- Store cheese by wrapping it in a piece of muslin or kitchen foil, and prevent mould from growing on it by wrapping it with a few sugar cubes.
- Hard cheese! To stop cheese from hardening around the edges, smear a little butter over them.
- Don't throw away any hard, left-over pieces of cheese, but instead grate them, mix in a little butter, season with some pepper, beat in a little dry sherry, transfer the mixture to a few ramekins, top with melted butter, et voila: potted cheese!
- To avoid cheese sauces ending up stringy, add the cheese to the sauce at the end of the cooking process and don't

Tasty and versatile, even the dry ends of cheese can be used in cooking.

then boil the sauce, but instead warm it over a gentle heat until all of the cheese has melted.
- Make your own, Greek-style yoghurt by first warming 1 litre (35 fl oz) of UHT or sterilised milk to blood heat and then gently stirring in the contents of a small pot of natural yoghurt. Pour the mixture into a warmed vacuum flask and screw on the lid tightly before leaving the flask in a warm place overnight. The next day, pour the yoghurt through either a fine sieve or a piece of muslin draped over a colander to separate the thick yoghurt from any liquid whey. (You could use the whey in cooking or could even wash your hair with it!) If you don't have any UHT or sterilised milk, you'll need to bring 1 litre of pasteurised milk to the boil, let it cool to blood heat and then continue with the method described above.

Ways with meat and poultry

The less exercised parts of animals produce the most tender meat, while the further it was from the animal's loin, the tougher the meat. Here are some more meat- and poultry-related tips.

- Tender meat is best cooked using a dry-heat method, such as oven-roasting or pan-frying. Tougher meat, on the other hand, is best cooked using a moisture-rich method, like stewing, braising or simmering slowly.

- Tenderise meat by hitting it with a rolling pin, but remember first to sprinkle a little cold water over the rolling pin and work surface to prevent the meat from sticking to them. Alternatively, squeeze a little papaya (pawpaw) or kiwi-fruit juice (which contains a tenderising enzyme) over the meat.

- Don't add salt to meat at the start of the cooking process because this will encourage the juices to escape from the meat, making it rubbery. Instead, season meat when it is cooked, just before serving it.

- When seasoning meat, sprinkle over the pepper (which is more expensive than salt) before the salt to ensure that the pepper adheres to the meat rather than falling off a steak, for example, that has just been salted.

- After you've browned minced beef, place a slice of bread over the top to absorb any excess fat.

Roasting meats on a rack in the oven will make the meat shrink less and won't overcook the base.

- If you roast a joint of meat by placing it on a rack in a roasting tin, there will be less shrinkage and the base won't end up being overcooked. If you don't have a roasting rack, roasting the joint on a bed of vegetables – such as celery, carrots and onions – will have the same effect of enabling the heat to circulate all around the meat, while the vegetables will give extra flavour to the pan juices when it comes to making gravy.

- When covering a joint of meat with kitchen foil, make sure that the foil is shiny side down so that the heat is reflected towards the meat rather than away from it.

- When it is cooked, leave a roast joint to stand on a hot dish at room temperature for at least twenty minutes before carving it to give the juices (which rise to the surface during the cooking process) time to settle back into the meat. Don't worry: placing it on a hot dish will ensure that the joint won't become cold.

- Rubbing a little vodka over a chicken before roasting it will make the skin crispy.

- Don't forget to season the cavity, as well as the skin, before roasting poultry.

- When grilling or barbecuing lots of sausages, save time by pushing them onto a long skewer or kebab stick to enable you to turn over a number at a time.

- To prevent bacon from tasting too salty, soak the rashers in warm water for fifteen minutes and then dry them off with a piece of kitchen towel before cooking them.

Once the only way to safely preserve meats, salting and smoking today is more about flavour.

- Prevent a gammon steak from curling by nicking the edges before cooking it.
- Placing a piece of stale bread in the grill pan will soak up any dripping fat, thereby preventing it from either smoking or catching fire.
- When turning chops and steaks, use tongs rather than a fork because if the fork pierces the meat, some of the tasty juices will escape.
- Before serving lamb, make sure that the serving plates are very hot to avoid the ugly sight of a plate swimming in congealed lamb fat.

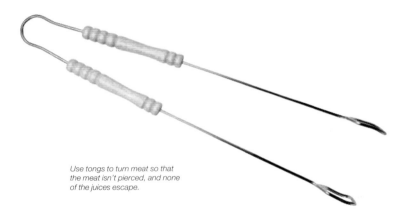

Use tongs to turn meat so that the meat isn't pierced, and none of the juices escape.

ROASTING TIMES FOR MEAT AND POULTRY

When roasting meat and poultry, refer to the timings and instructions given below.

ROASTING TIMES FOR PORK

Thirty-five minutes per 450 g (1 lb), plus thirty-five minutes.
Roast pork at 220°C (425°F/gas mark 7) for fifteen minutes, then turn down the heat to 180°C (350°F/gas mark 4) and continue cooking until the juices run clear when the meat is pierced with a skewer.

ROASTING TIMES FOR LAMB

Medium rare: ten minutes per 450 g (1 lb), plus ten minutes.

Medium: twenty minutes per 450 g (1 lb), plus fifteen minutes.

Well done: thirty minutes per 450 g (1 lb), plus thirty minutes.

Roast lamb at 220°C (425°F/gas mark 7) for fifteen minutes, then turn down the heat 180°C (350°F/gas mark 4) for the remaining cooking time.

ROASTING TIMES FOR BEEF

On the bone

Rare: fifteen minutes per 450 g (1 lb), plus fifteen minutes.

Medium: twenty minutes per 450 g (1 lb), plus twenty minutes.

Well done: twenty-five minutes per 450 g (1 lb), plus twenty-five minutes.

Off the bone

Rare: twelve minutes per 450 g (1 lb), plus twelve minutes.

Medium: fifteen minutes per 450 g (1 lb), plus fifteen minutes.

Well done: twenty minutes per 450 g (1 lb), plus twenty minutes.

Roast beef at 220°C (425°F/gas mark 7) for fifteen minutes, then turn down the heat to 180°C (350°F/gas mark 4) for the remainder of the cooking time.

ROASTING TIMES FOR CHICKEN

Twenty minutes per 450 g (1 lb), plus twenty minutes.

Roast chicken at 200°C (400°F/gas mark 6) until the juices run clear when the bird is pierced with a skewer.

ROASTING TIMES FOR DUCK

Thirty to thirty-five minutes per 450 g (1 lb).

Start by roasting duck on a rack at 180°C (350°F/gas mark 4), then turn up the heat to 200°C (400°F/gas mark 6) for the final twenty minutes, basting occasionally.

ROASTING TIMES FOR TURKEY

Oven-ready weight	Servings	Cooking time With foil	Without foil
2.3–3.6 kg (5–8 lb)	6–10	3–3 1/2 hours	2–2 1/2 hours
3.6–5 kg (8–11 lb)	10–15	3 1/2–4 hours	2 1/2–3 hours
5–6.8 kg (11–15 lb)	15–20	4–5 hours	3 1/4–3 3/4 hours
6.8–9 kg (15–20 lb)	20–30	5–5 1/2 hours	3 3/4–4 1/4 hours
9–11.3 kg (20–25 lb)	30–40	do not use	41/4–4 3/4 hours

Roast turkey at 180°C (350°F/gas mark 4). If the bird is not self-basting, brush it with oil or butter or spread strips of streaky bacon over the breast to keep it moist. Wrapping the bird in foil will reduce the need for basting because the foil keeps in more of the natural juices. Foil-wrapping does, however, increase the cooking time. In addition, remember that you must remove the foil for the last thirty to thirty-five minutes of cooking to allow the skin to brown. Note that birds weighing between 9 and 11.3 kg (between 20 and 25 lb) and more should not be cooked in foil.

Ways with fish

Make the most of fish by observing the following guidelines.

- You can tell if a lobster is fresh if it has a stiff tail.
- You'll find it easier to open a tin of sardines (or corned beef) if you turn the tin upside down and use a tin-opener rather than the key provided.
- Anchovies are very salty little fishes, so soak them in milk for an hour or so before serving them to draw off some of their saltiness.
- It is said that thawing frozen fish in milk gives it a more 'freshly caught' taste than simply defrosting it.
- Making a series of slashes about 2.5 cm (1 in) apart in the skin of both sides of oily fish, such as herrings, before grilling them will enable the fish to cook both more evenly and more quickly.
- Baking fillets of fish on lettuce leaves will ensure that the fish won't stick to the baking tray and will also keep it moist.

Nutritious and delicious, fish is available fresh, frozen and canned.

Clever substitutes

Running out of a vital ingredient happens to all of us, but needn't be a disaster if you know how to cheat.

- Emulate the flavour of sherry by combining rose and almond extracts.
- Create a pistachio flavor by mixing vanilla and almond extracts.
- Is the only lemon in your kitchen dried and shrivelled? If so, put it in a bowl, cover it with boiling water and let it stand for five minutes before squeezing out the juice.

- One egg short? If you need that extra egg for a cake whose ingredients include either a raising agent or self-raising flour, note that you can replace the egg with 15 ml (1 tablespoon) of any type of vinegar without the end product being adversely affected.
- If you've run out of milk for baking, peel and liquidise 700 g (1 1/2 lb) of courgettes; the resulting liquid can be substituted for about 2 cups of milk. (This is also a helpful hint if you find yourself having to feed strict vegans!)
- Make double cream go further by adding one egg white for every 300 ml (10 fl oz) of cream before whipping it.
- No buttermilk? Simply substitute 175 ml (6 fl oz) of natural yoghurt and 50 ml (2 fl oz) of milk.
- Make your own crème fraîche by first mixing 300 ml (10 fl oz) of soured cream with 450 ml (15 fl oz) of double cream. Cover the mixture and leave it to stand at room temperature for a couple of hours, or until it thickens, before refrigerating it. (Note that using UHT milk won't work.)
- Make single cream by gently heating (not boiling) 125 g (4 1/2 oz) of unsalted butter and 300 ml (10 fl oz) of milk. When the ingredients have melted together, transfer the mixture to a liquidiser and blend for ten seconds before leaving it to cool, stirring occasionally.
- Slightly under-ripe soft cheeses, such as Brie and Camembert, can be artificially ripened by popping them in the microwave for fifteen to twenty seconds on the defrost setting.
- Caster sugar is often called for in cake recipes, but if you don't have any, grind up some ordinary white, granulated sugar in a food processor or blender for a few seconds on a high-speed setting.
- Run out of coffee filters? Use a clean J-cloth or a couple of sheets of paper kitchen towel instead.
- Can't get the lid off a jar? Try snapping a wide rubber band around the lid and then twisting it off.

WARDROBES AND LAUNDRY

L ooking after your clothes properly not only means that you'll always look your best, but you'll prolong the life of the garments as well.

Whether you wash your clothes by hand or by machine, it's important to make sure that you match the correct washing procedure to the type of fabric. Depending on how dirty your laundry is, you'll also need to think about the correct water temperature, the type of detergent that you should use and how you should dry, iron and store your clothes and other laundry items after washing them.

CARE LABELS

Whenever you add a new item of clothing to your wardrobe, look for its international textile-care label, which you should find sewn into the waistband, neck or arm of the garment and which will give you the best advice about how to care for it, be it by dry-cleaning,

International textile care labels give all the instructions for looking after your laundry.

washing, drying or ironing it. Some detergent packaging also gives comprehensive information, which you could cut out of an empty box and keep for future reference.

THE SYMBOLS ON CARE LABELS FALL INTO FIVE CATEGORIES:

- washing symbol;
- bleaching symbol;
- drying symbol;
- ironing symbol;
- dry-cleaning symbol.
- Note that if any symbol has an 'X' through it, this treatment should be avoided.
- Use the care labels to guide you when shopping for clothes. Will a garment labelled 'dry-clean only' be practical for you? Will it spend more time at the cleaner's than you will spend wearing it? If it says 'hand-wash only', and you know you'll be putting it into the washing machine along with everything else, think hard before buying it.
- It's best to avoid removing the care labels from clothes, but if you find that one is visible or that it scratches, tickles or generally irritates you, cut it off, stick it onto a card and write down a description of the relevant garment next to it so that you will know how to care for it when the time comes.

Washing symbols

The washing symbol indicates that an item can be safely washed in the washing machine. If there is a bar beneath the symbol, a reduced washing time is indicated, as well as a reduced level of agitation for synthetic or delicate fabrics like silk and wool.

WASHING SYMBOLS

Symbol	Meaning	Fabric examples
95	Temperature 95°C. Wash using cotton programme. High temperature and maximum wash/spin ensure whiteness.	White cottons and linens without special finishes.
60	Temperature 60°C. Wash using cotton programme. A vigorous wash at a temperature that maintains colour-fastness.	Cottons, linens or viscose fabrics without special finishes where colours are fast at 60°C.
50	Temperature 50°C. Wash using synthetics programme. The reduced machine action and lower temperature preserve finish. The cold rinse and short spin minimise creases.	Polyester/cotton mixtures; nylon, polyester, cotton and viscose items with special finishes; cotton/acrylic.
40	Temperature 40°C. Wash using cotton programme. The low temperature prevents the colour from running.	Cotton, linen or viscose items where colours are fast at 40°C, but not at 60°C.
40	Temperature 40°C. Wash using synthetics programme. The gentle wash and spin maintain colour and shape and minimise creases.	Acrylics and acetates, including mixtures with wool; polyester/wool blends.

Symbol	Meaning	Fabric examples
40	Temperature 40°C. Wash using wool programme. The reduced machine action preserves the colour, shape and size of machine-washable woollen garments.	Wool, wool mixed with other fibres, and silk where the label indicates 'machine-wash'.
	Hand-wash only. Do not machine-wash.	Wool, silk, cashmere and other delicate fabrics.
	Do not wash.	See 'Dry-cleaning symbols', below.

BLEACHING SYMBOLS

Symbol	Meaning	Fabric examples
△	You can use chlorine (household) bleach.	White cotton.
	Do not use chlorine (household) bleach.	Coloured garments.

DRYING SYMBOLS

Symbol	Meaning	Fabric examples
	Can be tumble-dried. Avoid over-drying and remove items promptly. Where dots appear in the symbol: two dots indicate the highest heat setting; one dot indicates a low heat setting.	Sheets, pillowcases, sweats and tracksuits.
	Do not tumble-dry.	Wool.
|||	Drip-drying recommended from soaking wet.	Fabrics with 'easy-iron' finishes.
	Hang on line after spin-drying.	[FABRIC EXAMPLE?]
—	Dry flat.	Hand knits.

IRONING SYMBOLS

Symbol	Meaning	Fabric examples
	One dot indicates a cool iron.	Acrylic, nylon and polyester.
	Two dots indicate a warm iron.	Polyester mixtures, silk and wool.
	Three dots indicate a hot iron.	Cotton, linen and viscose.
	Do not iron.	Some synthetics.

DRY-CLEANING SYMBOLS

Symbol   Meaning

Ⓐ○ If the symbol has an 'A' in its circle, either have the garment professionally dry-cleaned or dry-clean it in a launderette dry-cleaning machine using any solvent.

Ⓟ A circle containing a 'P' indicates to a dry-cleaner that many types of solvent can be used on the garment. As well as being professionally dry-cleaned, it can be cleaned in a launderette dry-cleaning machine.

Ⓟ A 'P' in a circle with a bar underneath indicates to a dry-cleaner that certain precautions are needed. Do not use a launderette dry-cleaning machine.

Ⓕ An 'F' indicates that only a certain number of specialist dry-cleaners will be able to deal with the garment. It also indicates the use of solvent 113, especially on delicate fabrics. If this symbol appears on a care label, show it to a dry-cleaner to make sure that they can handle this type of work.

⊗ Do not dry-clean or press.

CAUTION

After dry-cleaning clothes yourself, or after having them dry-cleaned, make sure that they have been well aired before putting them away because the fumes that arise from dry-cleaning solvents can be quite toxic. Do not dry-clean any padded materials, duvets or anything that is likely to house the fumes for very long yourself. And when taking dry-cleaned items home in a car, make sure that at least one window is open to allow the fumes to escape.

Machine-washing preparations

Before washing anything, sort your laundry into appropriate piles – white cottons and linens, for example, or nylons and synthetics, silks and rayon items and woollens and non-colourfast items – to be washed separately. Following some further tips will avert a washing disaster, too.

- Secure zips and fastenings to prevent them from snagging on fabrics.
- Empty pockets of tissues (or else you'll end up with bits of paper stuck to everything), money and other oddments.
- Remove any belts and other non-washable items.
- Turn down the cuffs of trouser legs and brush off any loose dirt. If possible, do the same for pockets – bits of fluff have a tendency to stick in the corners.

White cottons and linens must be washed separately from coloured items to prevent colour runs.

Wash coloured towels separately for the first few washes to ensure that any excess dye doesn't stain other items in the wash.

- To test whether a garment is colour-fast, sandwich it between two pieces of white fabric and then run a steam iron over a small section. If any dye is transferred to the white fabric, then the garment is not colour-fast and should be hand-washed.
- Check items for any unusual stains and for seams that have come apart. Make any repairs before laundering because a washing-machine's action can cause small tears to become larger ones. Sew on any loose buttons, too, to prevent them from being pulled off in the wash, tearing the fabric and becoming lost in the washing machine.
- Turn corduroy and textured garments inside out to prevent them from picking up a bloom of fibres shed by other garments in the wash.
- Don't overload your washing machine: clothes will come out cleaner if there is room for them to circulate freely.
- Prevent tangling by attaching sleeve cuffs to the buttons on the fronts of shirts and blouses.
- If you load items into the washing machine one at a time, they won't come out too tangled. Put scarves, tights, stockings and bras into a net laundry bag (or improvise by making one from a piece of net curtain or even a pillowcase) to prevent them from snagging on, and becoming attached to, other garments.
- Use the right detergent for your wash, as well as the correct quantity. The ideal amount will vary according to the load size, the water hardness, the amount of water used and your laundry's dirt level. Follow the instructions either supplied with your washing machine or stated on the detergent package.

Finally, don't forget that if it is to do its job properly and efficiently, your washing machine itself needs to be clean. Although you could buy a proprietary cleaner – similar to a dishwasher cleaner – to run through the machine, pouring 4.55 litres (a gallon) of distilled vinegar into the machine and running it on a warm-water cycle and then a rinse cycle will cut through the built-up soap residue that can leave a bloom on clothes and that is especially noticeable on black and dark-coloured garments.

Don't forget to keep your washing machine clean as well!

Hand-washing tips

Although the general rule is that silk, woollen and hand-knitted garments should be washed by hand, any item that is machine-washable can be hand-washed as well. Indeed, it is often quicker and more economical to hand-wash two or three items than to run a cycle on a washing machine. When hand-washing, observe the following guidelines.

- If you have sensitive skin, wear rubber gloves.
- Dissolve detergents in warm water (unless a care label specifies cold water) before adding the clothes.
- If you find that you've got too many suds, reduce them by sprinkling a little talcum powder over them.
- Gently squeeze the water through the garments and avoid rubbing, twisting or wringing them, especially if they are made of wool.
- Rinse garments thoroughly – two or three rinses until the water runs clear is normally sufficient.
- Gently squeeze out the excess water. To remove more, either wrap hand-washed garments in towels or place delicate items in a pillowcase and give it a short spin in the washing machine.

- Washing them inside a pillowcase will protect delicate lace or 'vintage' garments. Lift and turn the pillowcase and squeeze the water through it before rinsing in the normal way.

- To avoid stretching them out of shape and putting undue stress on the seams, don't lift garments out of a sink, bowl, basin or bath when they are soaking wet.

- Adding two sugar lumps to the rinsing water will restore body to silk garments; adding a little lanolin to the rinsing water will also protect and restore silk; while adding a dash of white-wine vinegar to the rinsing water gives silk extra crispness (a friend in Moscow told me that's why little Russian girls' hair ribbons keep their bow shapes so perfectly).

Clothes hung up neatly in a wardrobe maintain their shape much better.

When to soak clothes

Soaking clothes prior to washing them loosens any dirt, as well as preserving colours by preventing fading.

A soap build-up causes black garments to develop a 'bloom' so that they no longer look black. Soaking them in warm water to which you've added a little white-wine vinegar will help to restore the blackness. Alternatively, replace the detergent in a regular machine wash with water-softener.

Although denim fades over time and through washing, new denim can sometimes shed some of its colour when it is first washed. To prevent new denims from fading, soak them for thirty minutes in a bucket, bath or basin filled with a solution of 5 litres (1.3 gallons) of water and 60 ml (4 tablespoons) of vinegar.

Preserve the bright hues of coloured clothes by soaking them in a bucket of water to which you've added a handful of salt before washing them for the first time.

Here are some more tips for successful soaking.

- Before putting clothes in to soak, completely dissolve powdered detergents in water.
- Try to keep garments immersed in the soaking water (the best soaking tub remains the bathtub).
- Soak stained items in hand-hot water for fifteen to twenty minutes or else in cold water overnight (perhaps in the bathtub).
- Don't soak woollen, leather, suede, Lycra or flame-resistant fabrics or garments that have metal trimmings (if you do, they'll rust).
- Don't soak garments with plastic buttons for too long because this can cause some plastics to disintegrate.
- Don't soak white and coloured items together because the dye in the coloured garments is likely to run and contaminate the whites.
- Before soaking them, test coloured fabrics for colour-fastness by dampening a little of the fabric in an unobtrusive spot (perhaps the inside of the hem or a seam allowance), placing a piece of white fabric over the top and then running a warm iron over it. If any colour is transferred to the white fabric, don't soak the coloured item, but instead take it to the dry-cleaners to be cleaned.

Whiter than white: bleaching

You can work wonders with household (chlorine) bleach if you know how to use it effectively. Always dilute bleach to avoid causing 'burns' in fabric. Although it's advisable to follow the manufacturer's instructions on dilution – which are usually given on the bottle – if in doubt, one good glug of bleach to a large bucketful of cold water usually works.

- Cotton and linen items can be soaked for short periods in a mild solution of household bleach and cold water.
- To restore the brightness of nylon items, fill a large bucket with very hot water and add 90 ml (6 tablespoons) of dishwasher detergent and 45 ml (3 tablespoons) of household bleach. Allow the mixture to cool to room temperature before soaking the items for at least thirty minutes.

- Rescue discoloured woollen items by soaking them overnight in a solution of 1 part hydrogen peroxide (available from chemists) to 8 parts cold water. Rinse the items thoroughly before washing them as advised by the care label.
- Not only is cream of tartar another good clothes-brightener, it is kinder to fabrics than many household bleaches. Add 2 tablespoons of cream of tartar to a bucket of hot water and leave the garments to soak in the solution overnight before washing them.

Make white cotton socks, pants, bras and other 'smalls' even whiter by placing them in a saucepan, filling it with water, adding a few slices of lemon and then boiling them, stirring them constantly with a clean wooden spoon.

Tackling spots and stains

Although most stains will come out of clothes if you act fast enough, many won't if you don't! Because laundering may cause stains to 'stick' – and once laundered, a greasy stain is almost impossible to remove – deal with them before washing the affected garment.

There are numerous pre-wash sprays, sticks and bars on the market, and if the fabric is suitable and the stain a protein-based one (such as those caused by food), another option is to soak it in an enzymatic detergent. You can also buy stain-spotting kits and grease solvents for 'dry-clean only' items.

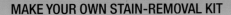

MAKE YOUR OWN STAIN-REMOVAL KIT

As an alternative to buying proprietary products, you could always make your own stain-removal kit. In addition to your usual laundry detergents, you will need some cotton-wool balls, a small, clean sponge, some large squares of clean, white cloth, such as old handkerchiefs or some shirts that you've cut up, and any of the substances listed below.

The following are my top tips for removing spots and stains.

- Be patient!
- Before doing anything, check the manufacturer's instructions on the care label.
- Try the simplest and gentlest solution first. Many stains will respond well to being soaked in a mixture of detergent and water, followed by a normal wash.
- Before using a stain-removal treatment, check that the fabric or finish will not be adversely affected by testing a small, invisible patch. If there is any colour change or the colour runs, consult a professional dry-cleaner.
- Never combine household (chlorine) bleach with other cleaning or stain-removal products because doing so may cause toxic gas to be generated.
- Use solvents sparingly and don't saturate the fabric with them.
- Apply a stain-removal solution to the back of the stain, that is, to the reverse side of the fabric, not to the front, to avoid driving the stain deeper into the fabric.
- When a stain has to be dipped into a solution, hold the fabric by the stained area and twist the unstained area (this will prevent the solution from spreading too far across the garment) before dipping the stained part into the solution.
- Using a proprietary stain-remover can leave what dry-cleaners call a 'sweal', or a round mark, that can be difficult to remove. To prevent this, when applying the stain-remover, use a dabbing rather than rubbing motion and work from the outside of the stain towards the centre to avoid

spreading it further. Professional dry-cleaners call this dabbing motion 'tamping', and although tamping takes time (which is one of the reasons why professional, good-quality dry-cleaning can be costly), it is advisable because repeated movements across the surface of the fabric can damage the structure of the threads, thereby leaving a permanent mark, even if the stain has itself been removed.

- After using a stain-removal treatment and then washing the garment, check to see whether the stain remains. If it is still there, repeat the treatment before tumble-drying the garment (if you intend to do so).

CAUTION

Note that because some of the chemicals listed below are either poisonous or flammable – or both – label their containers carefully and store them safely out of children's reach. In addition, never use these chemicals near a naked flame and make sure that the room in which you're working is well ventilated.

Ammonia

Ammonia is a very useful stain-removing aid that must be used in dilute form. A dilution of 1 part ammonia to 3 parts water is the most usual, although some stains require only a drop or two of neat ammonia to be added to the washing or rinsing water. Because fabric is prone to colour-bleeding when ammonia is used, make sure that you test for colour-fastness before treating a stain. Caution: ammonia gives off very unpleasant fumes and can burn the skin if it comes into contact with it in its neat form, so handle it with care.

Amyl acetate

Although amyl acetate resembles nail-varnish remover, it is safer to use on acetate fabrics. It will also dissolve some paints, glues and nail varnishes. Caution: amyl acetate is flammable.

Dry-cleaning fluid

Dry-cleaning fluid is very effective when it comes to removing grease stains of any kind. It can be bought as a 'dab-on' applicator that is gently dabbed onto grease stains, but test the fabric for colour-fastness first, don't use it on acetates, follow the manufacturer's instructions and avoid inhaling the fumes. Caution: proprietary solvents can dissolve some rubbers and plastics and can cause skin irritation, too, so handle them with care.

Eucalyptus oil

Eucalyptus oil is highly efficient at getting rid of tar stains (and is safe to use on animals, too).

Glycerine

Available from chemists, glycerine lubricates and softens dried-in stains. Dilute 1 part glycerine to 2 parts water, apply the solution to the stain and leave it for one hour before laundering the garment.

Hydrogen peroxide

A gentle bleach, hydrogen peroxide is recommended for treating food and dye-based stains. Available from chemists, it is sold in 'volumes' that indicate its strength; ask for 20 volume, make up a dilute solution of 1 part hydrogen peroxide to 6 parts water, soak the stain for thirty minutes, or until it has disappeared, and then launder the garment as normal. Because it is a bleach, always test a small patch of fabric first to ensure that the colour remains unaffected.

Lemons

Lemon provide an antidote to such stains as iron mould.

Methylated spirits

Methylated spirits (try to obtain the colourless type, available from chemists)

should be applied to stains with a cotton-wool pad. Although it is unlikely to strip away a garment's colour, always test it on an inconspicuous patch of fabric first. Do not use meths on acetate or triacetate fabrics. Caution: meths is both poisonous and flammable.

Proprietary pre-wash stain-removers

You'll find a number of proprietary pre-wash stain-removers in the shops, which are sold in small bottles, are well worth investing in if you care about your clothes, designed as they are to deal effectively with almost every imaginable stain, from blood and food stains through stains made by ball-point pens and lipsticks, to mystery stains of unknown origin. Take care when selecting which solvent to use on which stain, and follow the manufacturer's instructions when using such products.

Salt

Salt removes blood and sweat stains from most materials and is also good at absorbing fruit stains.

White spirit

White spirit will remove some paint stains. Caution: this substance is both flammable and very poisonous.

White-wine vinegar

A 'miracle-working' household standby, white-wine vinegar is ideal for removing perspiration stains. Use 15 ml (1 tablespoon) of white-wine vinegar to 250ml (1/2 pint) water.

AN EXPERT GUIDE TO STAIN-REMOVAL

If you don't have any of the stain-removers listed above to hand, here are some alternative, stain-specific tips. Note that they are all for use on washable fabrics and that you should always use caution and discretion.

Beer, ale and stout stains

- Beer, ale and stout stains should first be sponged with clean water, after which the stain should be treated with a solution of 1 part white-wine vinegar to 5 parts water (but don't use this on acetate fabrics). Rinse well, then soak the stain in a biological detergent and rinse again. If this method fails, try a solution of 1 part 20 volume hydrogen peroxide and 6 parts cold water, but colour-test a piece of the fabric first. Old stains can sometimes be removed with methylated spirits, followed by a wash in the hottest water that the fabric can stand.

Wine stains

- Wine stains need to be treated immediately. Soak white-wine stains with soda water, blot up the excess liquid with paper towels and then launder the fabric. Douse red-wine stains with white wine and then treat the fabric in the same way as for white-wine stains. If no white wine is to be had, however, sprinkle salt over red-wine stains and wash the garment in a solution of cold water and detergent. If the stain remains, try dabbing on a paste of cream of tartar and water and again wash the fabric in a solution of cold water and detergent.

Coffee and tea stains

- Fresh coffee stains can be removed by applying a mixture of egg yolk and glycerine to the stained area and then laundering the fabric in lukewarm water (not hot water, otherwise you'll end up with a cooked-on egg stain!)

- Dried-on tea stains should be softened with a solution of equal amounts of glycerine and warm water before being soaked in a biological detergent. If the stain still remains after laundering, try a little methylated spirits. To banish tea stains from white cotton completely, it may be necessary to bleach them.

Fruit and fruit juice

- To remove fruit and fruit-juice stains, sprinkle some salt over the stain, rinse it in cold water and then launder the fabric in warm water to which you've added a little detergent. If the stain persists, try treating it with a little hydrogen peroxide.

Curry and turmeric stains

- It'll be difficult to get rid of a curry or turmeric stain completely, so good luck! Try rubbing the stain with a mixture of 3 tablespoons of glycerine and 4 tablespoons of warm water and then leave it for an hour before laundering the fabric in warm water. If that doesn't work, try soaking the stain in a solution of ammonia diluted with water and resolve to wear a bib the next time that curry's on the menu!

Tomato sauce

- To remove tomato-based stains, try rubbing a generous amount of foamy shaving cream into the stain with your fingers, rinsing the fabric and then laundering it.

Chewing gum

- First pick off as much chewing gum as possible, then put the garment in a plastic bag and place it in the freezer for an hour or so, after which the gum should break off easily. Remove any remaining traces by either soaking them in white-wine vinegar or rubbing them with a little egg white before laundering the garment.

Blood stains

- As soon as a blood stain occurs, dab it first with a little soda water and then apply a paste made of cornflour and water before laundering the garment. Alternatively, immediately soak the stain in strongly salted cold water (don't use hot water because this will seal in the stain), keep changing the 'brine' until the water runs clear and then rub any remaining marks with a paste made of salt and water.
- You can sometimes remove dried-on blood by gently rubbing it with a sponge to which you've applied some foamy shaving cream. Soak really obstinate stains in a solution of 10 ml (2 teaspoons) ammonia, 500 ml (1 pint) water and a few drops of hydrogen peroxide and follow that with a wash using a biological detergent.

Candle wax

The best way of removing candle wax is to put the garment into the freezer – this will harden the wax, enabling you easily to break it off in pieces.

Alternatively, sandwich the wax-stained fabric between two clean pieces of blotting paper or towelling fabric and press it with a warm iron, shifting the blotting paper or towelling around so that it absorbs the wax. Use a dry-cleaning solvent to flush out any remaining wax and methylated spirits (diluted with an equal quantity of water for rayon and nylon fabrics) to rid the fabric of the candle's residual colour. Finally, wash the garment in the hottest water it can stand.

Bird droppings

- Birds always seem to 'plop' on clean shirts when you're on your way to work or on clean sheets that are drying on a clothes line! All that you can do is to scrape off the dropping, sponge the stain with salty water and then soak the fabric in a biological detergent.

Collar 'rings'

- Shirt collars and cuffs inevitably become grimy, but ironing laundered white cotton shirts and blouses with a little spray starch will help to lessen dirt adhesion and staining. Lightly spraying starch over pillowcases also prevents grease from make-up and facial cleansers from embedding itself in the fabric.

- Remove the rings of grime around collars and cuffs by first rubbing a piece of damp soap or stick of pre-wash proprietary stain-remover along the mark, making sure that it is thoroughly covered. Then, using a soft, wet toothbrush, work the soap into a lather, rinse the fabric in warm water and launder the item as normal. Another way of removing the ring of dirt around a collar is to work a paste made of bicarbonate of soda (baking soda) and white-wine vinegar into the mark with either your fingers or a soft toothbrush before laundering the shirt or blouse.

- Alternatively, because collar rings are caused by dirt adhering to the oil that the skin has deposited on the collar, try rubbing a little of your normal shampoo over the ring to loosen the oil and dirt before laundering the shirt or blouse as usual. You could also try outlining the collar ring with chalk, which will absorb the oil, although this method may require several applications. A final, ancient laundering tip is to clean a collar by rubbing a heel of white bread along it.

Grass and mud stains

- To remove grass stains, gently rub them with lemon juice before washing the garment.
- In the case of mud stains, first allow the mud to dry, then brush it off and work the fabric between your hands to remove as much dried mud as possible before laundering the garment. Remove dried-on mud stains by rubbing them with a raw potato, soaking the garment in cool water for a while and then laundering it in the usual way.

Iron mould

- Remove light iron-mould stains by rubbing lemon juice and salt into the mark, leaving the mixture on for about an hour and then rinsing the fabric well. Repeat if necessary.

Make-up stains

- First remove any excess make-up and then pat the stain with some talcum powder to soak up any grease. Treat light stains with a mixture of detergent and warm water, and heavier ones by soaking them in a solution of 5 ml (1 teaspoon) ammonia and 500 ml (1 pint) lukewarm water before laundering the garment.

Lipstick on your collar: while the colour is relatively easy to remove, it's the grease mark that needs the treatment.

- If the culprit was lipstick, scrape off any excess with a knife and then rub a little glycerine – or even some petroleum jelly, but if the fabric is nylon, use methylated spirits instead – into the stain to loosen it. If the mark shows no sign of disappearing, follow this treatment with a proprietary stain-remover or grease solvent and then launder the garment.
- To remove mascara stains, rub in a little neat washing-up liquid, then launder the garment as usual. If the stain remains, treat it with a dry-cleaning fluid.
- Deal with nail-varnish spills by blotting up as much as possible and then treating the back of the fabric with either some amyl acetate or a non-oily nail-varnish remover, followed by a little white spirit. If necessary, remove any remaining colour with some methylated spirits (but not if the fabric is acetate).

Pen stains

Marks made by ball-point pens can be significantly reduced by taking an ordinary rubber to them, using a gentle, circular action.

- Soap is by far the safest solution: rub a block of moistened soap over the mark, press the lather through the stain with your fingers until it starts to shift, then rinse it with lukewarm water. If this doesn't work and the fabric is white, try rubbing the stain with a mixture of lemon juice and salt and then, if possible, hang the garment out to dry in a sunny place. Ink stains can be removed from coloured fabrics by soaking the garment in hot, sour milk before laundering it (it may be a slow process, but it works).

A little hairspray will often lift off a felt pen mark.

- Deal with stains made by felt-tip or marker pens by spraying on a little hairspray before laundering the garment (but do a spot-test first to make sure that the hairspray won't adversely affect the fabric or, indeed, make its own stain).

Perfume stains

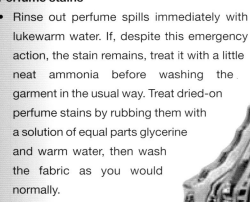

- Rinse out perfume spills immediately with lukewarm water. If, despite this emergency action, the stain remains, treat it with a little neat ammonia before washing the garment in the usual way. Treat dried-on perfume stains by rubbing them with a solution of equal parts glycerine and warm water, then wash the fabric as you would normally.

Perspiration and antiperspirant stains

- Freshen-up perspiration-stained clothes by dissolving a couple of crushed aspirins in the water in which you intend to wash them.
- Remove antiperspirant stains by applying a paste of bicarbonate of soda (baking soda) and salt, leaving it on for 30 minutes, soaking the garment in a biological detergent and then laundering it as usual.

Mystery stains of unknown origin

- First rinse the stain with cold water, then apply a pre-wash treatment and rinse it again. Next, launder the garment in water that is as hot as the fabric will stand, adding a little bleach if it is suitable for the fabric, before letting the garment air-dry (don't tumble-dry it in case the fabric is stained with grease). If the stain remains, soak the garment in cold water for one hour, apply a dry-cleaning solvent and rinse; repeat this procedure if the stain wasn't removed the first time around. If all else fails, try brushing a little white toothpaste over the stain with a toothbrush, rinsing and then laundering the garment (this sometimes works!)

An old toothbrush comes in handy for treating small areas of stain on clothes.

Drying tips

The following suggestions will help you to dry your clothes perfectly.

- Before drying laundered items, remove as much water as possible by spinning them in the washing machine or wringing them by hand.
- When drying laundered items, separate coloured fabrics from whites until you are sure that they are completely dry.

Woollen garments dry best when laid flat. Gently pull them into shape while they are still damp.

✿ ✿

- Leave woollens to dry naturally and don't expose them to heat or strong sunlight.
- Don't air linen in an airing cupboard for too long, otherwise you'll find yellow marks along the folds.
  To maintain your tumble-drier's efficiency, clean its filters frequently.
  When loading your tumble-drier, be guided by bulk rather than weight.
- Don't overfill your tumble-drier, for if you do, your washing will take longer to dry and your electricity bill will be higher as a result.
- Note that tumble-drying small and large items separately will enable them to dry faster.
- Don't tumble-dry light, fluffy garments with dark ones, otherwise the light fluff will be transferred to the dark clothes.
- Make sure that everything you put in your tumble-drier can take the heat (plastic fastenings, for example, may melt).
- Unloading your tumble-drier as soon as the cycle has finished will prevent dried items from becoming too crumpled. If you don't intend to iron them straightaway, hang them up.
- If tumble-dried clothes have become too dry to iron, return them to the tumble-drier with a wet towel and set the drier to run on a cool cycle.
- Before hanging out your laundry, wipe the clothesline, both to remove any water droplets and to clean it.
- Peg clothes to clotheslines by their strongest parts: for instance, peg skirts by the waistband, but trousers by the ankles (the weight of the waistband will help to smoothe out any creases, so that the trousers will require less ironing).
- Turn white garments inside out before pegging them to a clothesline so that if they catch any flying dirt, it'll be invisible when they are next worn.
- If you prefer to finish drying a woollen sweater on a clothesline, thread the legs of a pair of nylon tights through the arms of the sweater, pull the tights' waistband through the sweater's neck and then attach clothes pegs to the

tights' feet and waistband. Doing this will prevent the sweater from ending up with marks or indentations.

- Note that if you peg laundry to a clothesline with your back to the wind, the damp clothes won't be able to flap back into your face!

- Anti-freeze your laundry! As long as the air is dry, clothes will dry outside on even the coldest of days. To prevent garments from freezing (which can weaken their fibres), add a handful of salt to the water for the final rinse.

Ironing laundry

When you switch on your iron, don't use it straightaway, but instead allow five minutes for it to reach the correct temperature (most irons heat up beyond the set temperature before adjusting themselves). In the meantime, sort your ironing into piles: one for items that require a cool iron, one for those that need a warm iron and one for garments that require a hot one.

Remember that the dots on an iron's dial correspond to the dots on a garment's care label. If you have a steam iron, for example, don't set it to the steam setting unless a garment's care label shows three dots within the iron symbol.

Note that there is a difference between pressing and ironing. When you press, you lift and lower the iron with a light touch; when you iron, on the other hand, you slide the iron back and forth in the direction of the fabric's grain without applying any pressure – the weight of the iron is enough.

The sole plate of the iron should be clean and smooth if it's to glide over your clothes.

Few things make a better impression than a freshly laundered and ironed shirt or blouse. The tried-and-tested method for ironing them is as follows (iron a dress in the same way, but start with its skirt).

- Start by ironing the inside of the cuffs, working from the outside to the inside edge to avoid ironing in creases at the seams. Iron the outside of the cuffs in the same way.
- Iron the sleeves: first the cuff-opening side, then the other side.
- Iron the reverse side of the collar, then the 'right' side, working from the outside edge inwards, towards the middle of the collar.
- Turn the shirt around, so that one shoulder lies over the narrow end of the ironing board, and iron across the shoulders.
- Iron the back of the shirt.
- Iron the shirt's two front panels.

Here are some more tips for easy and effective ironing.

- Keep your iron clean and remove any sticky patches from the base by rubbing the iron backwards and forwards over a sheet of paper sprinkled with salt.
- A steam iron will become less furred up if, like your kettle, you empty it of water when you've finished using it. If it does become furred up, partially fill the iron with vinegar, turn it on and leave it to steam the vinegar away before repeating the process with distilled water.

Like kettles, irons can become furred with limescale, which can be removed with vinegar.

- You'll find having a special holder for your iron useful: not only will it prevent the iron from being knocked over accidentally, but you won't need to leave the iron standing upright while it cools.

- If you dislike ironed creases in the sleeves of shirts or blouses, especially if they are made of delicate fabrics, either invest in a sleeve board (a mini-ironing board designed especially for sleeves) or improvise by rolling up a hand towel, inserting it into the sleeve to give it shape and then ironing around it.
- Adjust the height of your ironing board so that you can work comfortably.
- Support large items like sheets on a chair while you're ironing.

- Reflect more heat onto your ironing by slipping some kitchen foil (shiny side facing upwards) underneath your ironing-board cover.
- Begin with items which require a cool iron first; increasing the temperature of your iron from cool to hot saves waiting for the iron to cool down and also reduces the risk of scorching those items that require a cooler iron.

- If the clothes that you're about to iron are too dry, dampen them by squirting them with water from a water-sprayer of the type used for misting houseplants.
- Fabric shine can be unsightly, so avoid creating it by ironing the reverse side of garments first and then the 'right' side (but only if necessary), and don't iron over fastenings, hems or seams.

- Iron trouser seams by smoothing them flat, then pressing the inside-leg seams, followed by the outside-leg seams.
- Don't iron over buttons, but instead iron around them (your iron should have a special groove at its tip that will enable you to do this easily).

- Don't iron over zips (plastic ones may melt, while metal ones may damage your iron's sole plate). Zip up the zip, turn the garment inside out and then, using just the tip of the iron, press the zip's inside flaps. Now unzip the zip and lightly press along the fabric into which the zip is set. Finally, zip up the zip again and press the fabric on the reverse side.
- As you're ironing it, move the garment away from you to prevent you from leaning on, and thus creasing, the section that you've just ironed.

- If you need to use a pressing cloth, use a piece of white cotton fabric, such as a piece of an old sheet or shirt.
- Before ironing a tie, slip a piece of shaped cardboard inside it to prevent the imprint of the under seam from appearing on the front.
- Ironing pleats in skirts often causes a shiny mark to be left on the fabric under the pleat. To avoid this, slip a length of thin cardboard under each pleat before ironing it.
- Press velvet on the reverse side through a thick cloth, such as a towel, to avoid flattening the pile, causing creases or the iron leaving outline marks. A stubborn crease in velvet is best dampened, held tight and then dried with a hair-dryer. Another alternative to ironing a velvet garment is to hang it in a steamy bathroom, which will encourage the creases to drop out.
- Embroidered items should be ironed on the reverse side with a towel placed beneath the embroidery to protect it from being crushed.
- Silk is best ironed when it is evenly damp (the exception is shantung, which should be bone-dry to prevent it from being marked). Select the iron's two-dot setting and then iron the silk item on the reverse side. To avoid causing iron marks, place a sheet of white tissue paper between the silk and the iron.
- Linen has an undeservedly bad reputation for being difficult to iron because once it is too dry, no amount of steaming or spraying

A dirty sole plate will leave marks on clean laundry. Clean the plate by rubbing over a sheet of paper sprinkled with salt.

with water will remove the creases. The secret is to iron linen when it's so damp that it's almost wet, when a hot iron will smoothe it beautifully.

- Press woollen items by placing a damp cloth over the garment, holding the iron in place for a few seconds, then lifting it and moving on to an adjoining section.
- Don't put away freshly ironed clothes immediately, especially if you've used a steam iron or a damp pressing cloth, but instead let them air for a bit. Similarly, don't put on a newly ironed garment straightaway because letting it 'cool off' for a bit will result in fewer creases.
- Don't hang clothes in wardrobes, or place them in drawers, that are too full because this will crush and crease your freshly ironed garments.

Trouser hangers which hold at the waistband make for fewer creases.

Storing clothes

Before putting away any clothes that you have just taken off, either give them a shake or brush them down to remove hairs and dust. And don't put clothes that should really be laundered into wardrobes or drawers, not least because stained clothes – especially woollen ones – will attract moths.

Here are some more ideas to help you keep your clothes in pristine condition.

- Hanging clothes on hangers while they are still warm from your body heat will encourage any creases to drop out.
- Give thought to your clothes hangers: wire hangers don't give full support to anything except the lightest clothes, but if you must use them, make them non-slip by winding a couple of rubber bands around each end. Invest in some

wooden hangers for jackets and shirts, as well as skirt or trouser hangers, which will prevent the centre of skirts or trouser legs from becoming creased.

Wooden and padded hangers offer better support for clothes than wire ones.

If you don't have a skirt hanger, cut a notch in each end of a wooden hanger to hold skirt loops securely.

- Don't hang woollen garments on hangers because they'll stretch and lose their shape.
- Don't hang up coats and jackets by the little loop that is often sewn inside the neck because it will pull the shoulders out of shape. Likewise, don't drape jackets over the newel posts of banisters or over the backs of chairs (that is, unless you want a hump in the back of your jacket or shoulders that point upwards!)
- Remove belts from coats and store them separately by hanging them by the buckle from a hook on the back of the wardrobe door.
- Encourage clothes to keep their shape while they're not being worn by doing up zips, fastening buttons or folding them carefully.
- Repair dropped hems and replace missing buttons as soon as you can.
- Wet clothes, such as raincoats and overcoats, should be allowed to dry naturally before being put away.
- Don't simply wring out swimsuits before putting them away. Because suntan lotion, salt water and the chlorine in swimming pools can all rot their fibres, rinse swimsuits by hand in clean water and then lay them out flat to dry. Don't leave wet swimwear in plastic bags either because this will cause it to rot.
- Pack away summer clothes in winter, and vice versa, but make sure that they are clean first.

Wrap white silk and other delicate materials in tissue paper to prevent the light from turning them yellow.

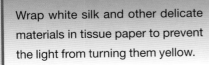

- Keep garments that are worn on very special occasions in perfect condition by covering them with a dress- or suit-cover. Hanging evening dresses inside out will keep them as clean as possible, while sewing long loops onto the waistband will take the strain off the shoulder seams when long dresses are hung on hangers.

- Don't store a wedding dress in an ordinary plastic or PVC bag or cardboard box because chemicals in such packaging can leach out over time, causing the fabric to become permanently discoloured, a reaction that is hastened if there is little or no air movement (which means that storing a wedding dress in a wooden trunk will have the same effect). You can buy special dress boxes made of acid-reduced cardboard, as well as acid-free tissue paper with which to line the box, to interleave between the folds of the dress and to insert into the bodice, sleeves, shoulders and any bows. Another option is to have your wedding dress vacuum-packed,

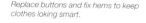
Replace buttons and fix hems to keep clothes loking smart.

which will prevent oxidisation and discolouration. Although vacuum-packing should preserve a gown for at least twenty-five years, you won't be able to take the dress out on a whim and it may end up being permanently creased. Consult your wedding-dress supplier or dry-cleaner for further advice and information.

Wedding dresses need special care to store them safely.

- Moths attack natural fibres, especially wool, as well as natural fibres that have been mixed with synthetics. To ward off a moth attack, make sure that clothes are clean before storing them in garment bags.

- To protect your clothes from moths, hang insecticidal strips or proprietary moth-repellants in your wardrobe. Alternatively, use a natural moth-repellant, such as cedar wood or lavender. Small cedar-wood blocks should be lightly sanded regularly to release their natural oil; lavender should be encased in muslin or cotton bags because lavender oil can itself burn holes in fibres. Citrus peel and whole cloves are also excellent moth-repellents: scatter the peel in wardrobes and drawers or pop whole cloves in coat pockets and among woollens before storing them away for the summer.

Cedar wood balls and cubes, rubbed with sandpaper release a natural oil which moths hate.

- Line drawers with paper to keep garments dust-free.

- If you store unwrapped scented soap in your drawers and linen cupboard, the soap will scent your clothes and linen, at the same time drying and hardening, which means that it will last longer when you come to use it.

Absorb any atmospheric dampness by tying some sticks of white blackboard chalk with a ribbon and hanging the bunch in your wardrobe.

Looking after shoes and boots

The following tips will prolong the life of your footwear.

- Liberally sprinkling the insides of shoes with bicarbonate of soda (baking soda) at night and emptying it out in the morning will ward off unpleasant foot odours.
- To prevent patent leather from drying and cracking, clean it frequently with a little creamy milk or petroleum jelly and finish by polishing it with a soft cloth.

A little petroleum jelly 'feeds' patent leather and stops it cracking.

- Patent-leather shoes are prone to developing lines and creases, so discourage this by using shoe trees or inserting balls of paper in the toes and holding them in place with spring sticks.
- The salt stains that can appear on shoes when roads have been salted in winter are very hard to remove. Although the salt will continue to emerge if the shoes have been completely soaked through, surface stains can be removed with a mixture of 1 part washing-up liquid, 1 part white spirit and 4 parts water. Work this creamy emulsion over the surface of the entire shoe, paying extra attention to the salt line, before rinsing the shoe and drying it gently. This should remove the polish and, with luck, the stain. Repolish the shoe when it is absolutely dry.

- Brush suede lightly, and in one direction only, otherwise it will look shaggy. Shiny, matted suede should be rubbed in one direction with a piece of coarse sandpaper.
- Clean canvas shoes with a toothbrush dipped in carpet-shampoo. Although most trainers can be washed in a washing machine, don't tumble-dry them and instead let them dry naturally.
- New shoes that are a little tight can be made more comfortable if you warm them slightly before putting them on. Shoes that really pinch can be stretched a bit if you hold the culprit area over the spout of a steaming kettle; when the area has started to become warm, shape it with the rounded end of a broom handle or the bowl of a spoon, then either put the shoes on and wear

Canvas shoes can be cleaned with carpet cleaner or an old toothbrush.

them in, or stuff them with newspaper to preserve the desired shape.
- If you think that a shoe or sandal strap is likely to chafe your foot, rub a little moist soap over the suspect part before putting the shoe on.
- Squeaks in men's new shoes are often caused by friction between the leather sole's two layers. Oiling the soles with linseed oil should cure the squeak when the oil reaches the point of friction. The oil also extends the life of the soles (but don't let him walk on any carpets in them for a while!) If a woman's shoe squeaks, it is usually because the metal arch support in the sole has worked loose. Fixing this is a job for a professional shoe-repairer.
- Don't allow the heels of your shoes to become so worn down that the heel itself is damaged.
- Avoid wearing the same shoes for two days running, partly to give your feet a rest from them and partly to enable the shoes to dry out and any odour to disappear.

- Stuff the legs of boots with rolled-up magazines or newspapers to encourage them to keep their shape.
- If shoes or boots become wet, stuff them with newspaper (this will absorb the moisture and will help them to keep their shape) and let them dry out naturally.
- Dry the insides of wet Wellington boots with a hair-dryer.

Caring for accessories

They say that accessories make an outfit, so take good care of yours.

- Keep handbags in shape when they are not being used by stuffing them with tissue paper. Store them either in the cloth bag in which they were sold or an old pillowcase.
- It is said that washing nylon tights and stockings in a mild soapy solution and not rinsing them makes them less likely to become snagged or laddered. Some people maintain that keeping them in the freezer, thawing them and then letting them drip-dry before wearing them doubles their life expectancy.
- Soaking silk stockings in the water in which bran has been steeped is said to prolong their life. For a really good fit, some people advocate soaking them in a mixture of vinegar and water.
- Stop ladders in nylon tights and stockings from becoming worse by either rubbing in a little moist soap or putting a dab of clear nail varnish on both ends of the run.
- If your beret becomes wet, place it over a dinner plate of the same size to prevent it from shrinking as it dries.
- Put on jewellery after you've finished dressing and applying perfume and make-up. Pearls and certain gemstones can be damaged by cosmetics and perfumes, while there is no surer way of snagging nylon tights than wearing rings on your fingers when you're putting them on.

Perfume can mark and stain clothes and damage precious jewellery, so apply it before you get dressed.

- If you are lucky enough to own a string of pearls, wear them as often as you can, even if they can't be seen – perhaps under a sweater – because your skin's natural oils will prevent them from drying out and cracking. Routinely check their stringing for signs of wear and have them restrung regularly to prevent accidental breakages.

- If your jewellery leaves marks on your skin, this will either be because tiny particles of metal or tarnish are flaking off it or because you are allergic to the metal. A short-term remedy is to clean the piece of jewellery and then to apply a thin coating of clear nail varnish to the part that comes into contact with your skin.

- Clean any jewellery that you wear frequently every five or six weeks, treating one item at a time so that hard stones don't damage softer ones. Don't clean your jewellery over the kitchen sink or bathroom basin – do it over a small bowl instead – in case rings, loose stones or the backs of earrings disappear down the plughole.

- If you use a proprietary jewellery dip, reserve it exclusively for your jewellery and don't clean cutlery in it because any metal that the dip may remove from the cutlery could then be deposited on your jewellery, damaging any gemstones.

LOOKING GOOD FROM HEAD TO TOE

Although ancient cultures across the world used perfumed oils for anointing their bodies, the first recipe for a 'beauty product' – a face cream – was recorded by the Greek physician Galen (c.130–200 AD), who attended the Roman emperor Marcus Aurelius. Like many of his medical writings, which continued to influence medicine right through the Middle Ages and beyond, Galen's recipe for a facial cream based on oil, water and wax has formed the basis of many of the 'day creams' that are in use today.

Today's commercial beauty products are often expensive, not because their ingredients are costly, but largely in reflection of the vast amounts of money that the manufacturers spend on promoting their brands through advertising and packaging, as well as their distribution costs. Running alongside the increased use of chemical preservatives, synthetic perfumes and colourants in such products is a rise in allergies, however, which has in turn resulted in an increased demand for natural ingredients and for products that have not been tested on animals.

Rather than spending a fortune on commercial products, why not make your own beauty preparations? Not only is this easy, but by doing so you'll know what they contain and can furthermore tailor their ingredients to suit your personal needs. For safety's sake, do bear in mind that if consuming a particular food causes you to break out in an allergic reaction, this is equally likely to happen if you apply it to your skin or hair. Remember, too, that just like the food that you put inside it, what you put on your body should be as fresh as possible. (Even shop-bought cosmetics and creams will begin to oxidise and go off once they've been opened, especially after someone's dipped a greasy or dirty finger into them.)

Most home-made beauty preparations are very simple, quick and inexpensive to make and use. Many contain fresh herbs, which are readily available from health-food stores and supermarkets; alternatively, you could grow your own selection in the smallest of gardens, a sunny window box or pots on a kitchen windowsill. (You'll find hints and tips for growing herbs and other plants and flowers in Chapter 6.) You can also use dried herbs, but if you do, use only half the quantity specified for their fresh counterparts.

No matter how much you spend on hair and beauty products, or how many you use, be warned that they will not compensate for the effects of a bad diet, too many late nights, not enough fresh air and exercise and the ravaging effects of smoking and drinking alcohol. The last two are perhaps the greatest destroyers of health and the ruin of many a complexion: alcohol dilates the blood vessels, opens pores in the skin and reduces muscle tone, while smokers have more – and deeper – wrinkles than non-smokers.

So if you want to improve your looks, first look to your diet and lifestyle and:
- quit smoking;
- cut alcohol, tea, coffee and cola drinks from your diet and instead drink herbal or fruit teas, fruit juices and mineral water – not only will you save a fortune by making the switch, but your skin and body will thank you;
- drink half a glass of water with a good squeeze of lemon in it first thing in the morning and last thing at night for bright eyes and a clear complexion.

KNOW YOUR SKIN TYPE

Although many consultants at the beauty counters in major department stores offer advice on skin types and appropriate treatments (albeit only the ones manufactured by the cosmetic companies that they represent), it's easy to identify your skin type yourself.

To do this, first wash and rinse your face thoroughly and then pat it dry with a towel. Wait for two hours – or overnight, if you prefer – and then press a paper tissue against your face. If the tissue comes away evenly covered with grease, you have oily skin. (Don't despair though: it is said that because oily skin is less sensitive to the sun and wind, it will appear supple and youthful for longer than other skin types.) If there is grease on certain parts of the tissue – usually the parts that came into contact with your chin and forehead – you have a combination skin. If the tissue comes away unmarked, wash your face with soap and water, and if your skin feels soft and supple afterwards, you have normal skin. (Why it is called 'normal' skin is one of life's mysteries because people rarely have it!) If, on the other hand, your skin feels taut, you have dry skin.

Don't think that because you had a particular type of skin during your teenage years it will remain the same during your twenties, thirties and later because hormonal, dietary and environmental changes cause the skin to change too, and it often becomes drier and more sensitive as we age.

The largest organ of our body – the skin – deserves special care to kept it working well and looking good.

Although your skin looks after itself naturally by shedding dead cells and replacing them with new ones, our polluted atmosphere, the effects of the weather and many women's habit of wearing make-up make regular cleansing one of the most important parts of the 'skin-maintenance' routine. Whatever your skin type, make sure that the cleansing process is gentle and take extra care when cleansing around the eyes, where the skin is thin and very sensitive. Avoid dragging the skin, and try to get into the habit of stroking one finger (but not your index finger, which is usually the strongest and grimiest because you use it the most) lightly up and across your face as you cleanse it.

A daily skincare routine

The daily routine for healthy-looking skin consists of cleansing, toning and moisturising.

Cleansing your skin

Soap emulsifies the protective oils on your skin, allowing them to be washed off with water. Although your skin will naturally replace these oils within hours, too much washing, or the use of strong soaps, can strip it of them. The more chemicals or perfumes a soap contains, the greater the danger that it will irritate your skin, so use the simplest sort of soap possible.

Cleansing creams are generally more efficient than soap at removing heavy dirt and make-up, which can lodge in pores and wrinkles, ageing the skin and making it look dull and lifeless. Follow this recipe to make your own cleansing cream for dry and normal skin types; all of the ingredients are available from chemists, herbalists and some health-food stores, too.

The first step in skin care is cleansing. No matter how late you get home, don't neglect your face!

- Melt 60 ml (4 tablespoons) of lanolin (a thick fat obtained from sheep's wool, which softens and nourishes the skin) in a glass bowl placed over a saucepan of simmering water.
- In a second saucepan, gently warm 50 ml (2 fl oz) of almond oil and 15 ml (1 tablespoon) of glycerine. Try to ensure that the ingredients in both pans are about the same temperature, then slowly pour the oil-and-glycerine mixture into the lanolin, all the while beating the lanolin constantly with a small whisk.
- In a bowl, dissolve a tiny quantity – just the tip of a teaspoon – of borax (a white, crystalline, mineral powder that functions as an emulsifier, which you could omit if you'd prefer the cleanser to have the consistency of a lotion rather than a cream) in 45 ml (3 tablespoons) of warmed rose water.
- Add the rose-water mixture to the lanolin mixture, beating the latter all the time, and then leave it to cool.
- When the mixture has become cool and creamy, beat in 5 ml (1 teaspoon) of zinc-oxide ointment (which has mild antiseptic and astringent qualities) and 6 drops of essential rose oil.
- Spoon the cream into a clean jar, label and date it, pop it into the refrigerator to keep it fresh and use it up within a few weeks.

Camomile cleansing milk is excellent for dry and sensitive skins. To make your own, simply heat 125 ml (1/4 pint) of creamy milk and 30 ml (2 tablespoons) of fresh or dried camomile flowers in a bowl set over a pan of simmering water for thirty minutes. Don't let the milk boil or a skin form. Remove the bowl from the heat and leave the milk to infuse for two hours before straining it. Transfer it to a jar or bottle and label and date it. Keep the cleansing milk in the fridge and use it up within a week. It should be applied to the skin with cotton wool and any excess should be gently wiped away with a paper tissue.

If your skin type is oily, try this buttermilk and fennel cleansing milk. Gently heat together 125 ml (1/4 pint) of buttermilk (or natural yoghurt) and 30 ml (2 tablespoons) of crushed fennel seeds in a bowl set over a pan of simmering water

for thirty minutes. Remove the bowl from the heat and leave the buttermilk to infuse for two hours before straining, bottling, labelling and refrigerating the cleansing milk, which should again be used up within a week.

Toning your skin

Toners, which are also called astringents, refreshers and tonics, remove the last traces of cleansing creams and lotions from the skin, as well as tightening the pores. They can also be used during the day as quick, refreshing cleansers.

A blend of rose water and witch hazel, shaken in a bottle before use, makes an excellent toner.

- Neat witch hazel (which is mildly antiseptic) makes a terrific and inexpensive toner. Buy it from your local chemist and dab it onto your skin with a cotton-wool ball. Alternatively, make a refreshing, pH-balanced toner by squeezing the juice of a lemon into a bottle of mineral water; not only can you dab it onto your skin after cleansing it, but you can drink it, too!
- One of the oldest toners, as well as one of the easiest to make, consists of 45 ml (3 tablespoons) of rose water (which softens the skin) and 15 ml (1 tablespoon) of witch hazel, blended in a bottle and shaken well before use. The proportions given above are suitable for normal skins; for greasy skins, use equal proportions of the two ingredients, while for dry skins, mix 45 ml (3 tablespoons) of rose water with 5 ml (1 teaspoon) of runny honey.

Cucumber is a good antidote to oily skins. To make a cucumber-based toner, whiz up a chunk of cucumber in a food processor or blender, strain the pulp by pushing it through a small tea-strainer with the back of a spoon, mix the cucumber juice with a few drops of honey and stir well. Transfer the toner to a bottle label it, store it in the fridge, where it will stay fresh for several days, and dab it on after cleansing your skin.

- A large handful of elder flowers makes an excellent toner. First bruise them by pounding them thoroughly, then transfer them to a bowl and pour over 500 ml (1 pint) of boiling water. Let the flowers steep in the water for two to three days, then strain off the liquid and squeeze the last drops of moisture from the flowers (and discard them). Lacking preservatives, this toner will not keep too well, so reserve a little of the liquid for use over the next two or three days and freeze the remainder in an ice-cube tray to make handy individual daily portions that you can melt as needed. If you don't have any elder flowers, use a bunch of parsley, or even a couple of pinches of dried parsley, which will benefit all skin types.

- If you suffer from spots, you can make a good antiseptic toner by substituting thyme for the elder flowers and following the instructions above. Whether you use elder flowers, parsley or thyme, if you want your toner to be a little more astringent, add a little witch hazel, or even a little cider vinegar, to help to restore your skin's pH balance, especially if you have cleansed it with soap.

Many herbs have uses in skin care, and can be a good, natural alternative to chemical treatments.

Moisturising your skin

The main function of a moisturiser is to maintain the skin's natural moisture level by forming a thin, protective film over it. It also protects the skin from the damage that can be caused by dirt and dryness in the atmosphere.

The best moisturiser for any skin is water. And while drinking plenty of water throughout the day is the best way of keeping your skin in tiptop condition, you can apply it directly to your skin as well. Fill a small atomiser with mineral water – mineral water seems to be more effective, if more expensive, than tap water – and keep it in your bag, car or desk at work to restore your face's vitality (but don't forget your neck!)

with a lightly misted spray of water. Keep your atomiser to hand on aeroplanes, too: because the air is recirculated around the cabin, your skin will quickly dry out, even on short-haul flights, but if you use your atomiser, you're more likely to arrive at your destination looking like a movie star than a piece of lost luggage.

Don't underestimate the value of water – as a drink or for bathing.

If you'd like to make your own moisturising cream, here's a recipe for one that's both light and suitable for all skin types.

- Melt 5 ml (1 teaspoon) of beeswax and 5 ml (1 teaspoon) of lanolin in a bowl set over a pan of simmering water, stirring constantly.
- In another bowl set over a pan of simmering water, gently warm 15 ml (1 tablespoon) of almond oil with 2.5 ml (1/2 teaspoon) of wheat-germ oil before gradually beating the oils into the wax mixture.
- Dissolve a little borax (about the tip of a teaspoon) in 45 ml (3 tablespoons) of warmed rose water and then slowly add the rose water to the wax mixture, beating continually until the mixture has cooled.
- As the mixture begins to thicken, stir in 6 drops of essential oil of rose. (If you'd like the cream to have a delicate rose colour, add a few drops of red food colouring, too.) Now spoon the cream into a jar, label and date it and store it in the fridge.

HERE ARE TWO FINAL MOISTURISING TIPS:

- applying a mixture of glycerine and rose water to a slightly wet face will seal in the moisture;
- if you have dry skin, rub the inner surface of some avocado skins over your face and neck (after you've enjoyed the tasty fruit, of course!)

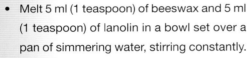

SPECIAL FACIAL TREATMENTS

Face masks have been used as beauty preparations for thousands of years: the ancient Egyptians were known to use crocodile dung, but there are fortunately lots more attractive – and easier to obtain – alternatives! The most important things to note about using face masks and scrubs is that they should be freshly made and should never be applied to the delicate skin around the eyes. Remember, too, that if you are allergic to any foods, applying them to your skin is also likely to cause an allergic reaction.

A special treat: a homemade face mask.

Facial saunas

Steaming your face over a steam bath opens the pores and encourages the skin to sweat out any impurities.

CAUTION

If you have broken veins on your face, don't have a facial sauna because it may worsen them.

To enjoy a facial sauna, add some lemon juice and mint leaves to a bowl of hot water, cover your head with a towel and then lean over the bowl, arranging the towel so that it prevents the steam from escaping. Close your eyes and steam your face for five minutes if you have oily skin, or for two minutes if you have normal or dry skin, breathing in the delicious scent of the lemons and mint. When your time's up, splash your face with cold water and pat it dry.

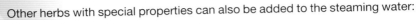

Other herbs with special properties can also be added to the steaming water:

- fennel for removing impurities;
- rosemary for deep cleansing;
- lavender, rose petals, thyme or camomile for gentle cleansing;
- sage for oily skins;
- parsley for dry or sensitive skins;
- dandelion leaves for older or sallow skins.

Exfoliation

The grains in facial scrubs exfoliate the skin by removing dead cells, thereby speeding up the growth of new ones and making the skin feel cleaner and softer and look fresher. Facial scrubs and masks, which should only be used occasionally, are widely available from chemists and beauty counters, but you can also easily make your own.

If you wish, you could add a little honey to any of the recipes below. When applied to the skin, honey both attracts and holds in moisture, and is also mildly antiseptic (it has been used to heal wounds since the time of the ancient Greeks). Older skins in particular seem to benefit from the addition of a little honey to face masks.

OATMEAL SCRUB

Oatmeal is both the oldest exfoliator and the best at sloughing off dead skin. Mix 30 ml (2 tablespoons) of coarse oatmeal with 5 ml (1 teaspoon) of honey and a little natural yoghurt to make a paste. Apply the paste to your face and neck – avoiding the delicate skin around the eyes – and then massage it in, using only your fingertips. Allow the paste to dry before rinsing it off with cool water.

Strawberry face mask

This is one of the easiest masks to make, and is also a good way of using up any bruised or squashed strawberries that you may find at the bottom of a punnet. Because strawberries are slightly astringent, they will tighten the skin, close open pores and smooth out fine lines. Simply mash up two or three strawberries, lie down and spread them over your face. (If you have dry skin, add 5 ml (1 teaspoon) of creamy milk.) Relax for fifteen minutes before rinsing off the strawberry mask with lukewarm water.

Yoghurt face mask

Make this mask, which is good for oily skins, by mixing some plain yoghurt with fuller's earth (a fine, grey powder, derived from single-cell algae found on sea beds, that has a rich mineral content and is highly absorbent) to a creamy constituency. Spread the mask over your face and relax for twenty to thirty minutes before rinsing it off with lukewarm water.

Cream and pear mask

Pears moisturise and nourish the skin, so if a pear in your fruit bowl has ripened too much, mash it with a little cream (or yoghurt), apply it to your face, relax for twenty minutes and then rinse it off with lukewarm water.

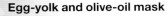

Egg-yolk and olive-oil mask

Being quite a heavy 'cream', this mask will soothe dry skins. To make it, lightly beat an egg yolk and then add 30 ml (2 tablespoons) of olive oil, a drop at a time. Apply the mask to your face, allow it to dry and then rinse it off with cool water.

Avocado and egg-white mask

This mask is suitable for normal skin types. Mash up a ripe avocado and then mix it with a squeeze of lemon juice and the white of one egg that has been beaten until it is frothy. Apply the mask to your face, allow it to dry and then rinse it off with cool water.

FULL BODY TREATMENTS

Pamper your body as well as well as your face!

Olive oil tastes good, and soothes the skin.

Milk bath

It's not quite Cleopatra's bath of asses' milk, but the milk softens the skin, while the lemon is astringent and cleansing. Squeeze half a lemon into 500 ml (1 pint) of whole (not skimmed) milk, apply the solution to your body with a sponge and leave it to dry for ten to fifteen minutes before rinsing it off with lukewarm water.

Oatmeal body mask

Mix together enough yoghurt and coarse oatmeal to cover your body, apply the paste to your skin, leave it on for fifteen minutes, shower it off with warm water and you'll be amazed how clean, toned and smooth your body feels.

✳ ✳

Herbal baths

Soaking in an aromatic herbal bath is one of the most pleasurable ways of treating and looking after your skin. You can use herbs to stimulate and invigorate or herbs to relax and soothe your body. You can use them to treat skin complaints or can simply enjoy their wonderful aroma. Note that your bath water shouldn't be too hot because the heat will make you perspire and your skin then

Relaxing in a warm bath at the end of a long day takes away stresses and strains.

won't be able to absorb the herbs' therapeutic agents (very hot water also ages the skin). Instead, relax in body-heat bath water for around ten minutes.

If you don't mind emerging from your bath looking like a swamp creature, sprinkle some herbs or flower petals over the water. Alternatively, make a herbal bath bag by placing your chosen herbs at the centre of a square of muslin or fine gauze and then tying up the edges, leaving long loops with which to hang the bag from the hot tap. You could also add a little oatmeal and use the bath bag as an exfoliating body rub. Dry your herbal bath bags after each use and discard them when their scent has faded.

Choose your therapeutic bath herb

- Healing (both body and spirit) bath herbs: calendula, comfrey, spearmint and yarrow.
- Relaxing bath herbs: camomile, jasmine, hops, valerian, meadow sweet and lime flowers.
- Stimulating and invigorating bath herbs: basil, bay, fennel, eucalyptus, lavender, lemon balm, lemon verbena, mint, pine, rosemary, sage and thyme.

A whole variety of herbs is available to suit or lift your mood.

Herbal infusions and essential oils

If you prefer not to make a herbal bath bag, you could extract the beneficial properties of your chosen herb by infusing 275 g (10 oz) of the dried herb – or a large handful of the fresh herb – in 500 ml (1 pint) of boiling water for ten minutes before straining the infusion, discarding the herbs and adding the liquid to your bath water.

You can also add five to ten drops of the herb's essential oil to your bath water. (Don't add essential oils to hot running water because they'll evaporate, but sprinkle them over the hot water after it has settled and then swirl it around to disperse them.)

HERE A FEW MORE BATH-TIME TIPS.

- To ensure that the essential oil is evenly dispersed in your bath water, mix it with 15 ml (a tablespoon) of milk.
- If you have dry skin, mix the essential oil with 15 ml (a tablespoon) of almond oil.
- To make an essential-oil bubble bath, along with the oil, add 15 ml (a tablespoon) of mild liquid soap or baby shampoo to your bath water.
- The harder a soap, the longer it will last. Remove the wrappers from newly bought soaps and tuck the bars between sheets and towels or among your lingerie. As well as scenting your linens, doing this will encourage the soap to harden, thus prolonging its working life.

THE EYES HAVE IT!

The finest recipe for bright eyes is a good night's sleep. Failing that, tired or irritated eyes can easily be soothed if you know how, but remember that it's essential to pay attention to matters of hygiene and cleanliness and not to rub your eyes with your fingers.

Eyes – and the skin around them, which is thin and delicate – need to handled with extra care. If anything irritates your eyes, avoid it. Eye make-up – eye shadow, eyeliner and mascara – should be fresh, so throw out your old products and treat yourself to some new ones. Remember that removing eye make-up is not a job to be rushed, especially if it's designed to be waterproof or long-lasting, and note that a little baby oil applied to cotton wool and gently swabbed over your eyelids will remove eye make-up just as effectively as any proprietary preparation or pad.

The best-known eye-brightener is a little plant called *Euphrasia rostkoviana*, commonly known in English-speaking countries as 'eyebright'. (The French delightfully call it *casse-lunette*, meaning 'throw away your spectacles', while the ever-poetic Italians know it as *luminella*, 'light for the eyes'.) A wonderful treatment for tired eyes, it's also soothing if you suffer from running eyes caused by hay fever. You can buy eyebright in dried form from good herbalists. To make an eyebright eyebath, boil 10 ml (2 teaspoons) of the dried herb in 450 ml (just under a pint) of water for twenty minutes. Leave the liquid to cool, strain it at least three times through a coffee-filter paper to remove any tiny particles of the herb and then use it immediately in an eyebath.

A simple, but effective, way of reducing puffiness around the eyes is to lie down, close your eyes, place a slice of cooling cucumber over each eye and then to relax, while dissolving 5 ml (1 teaspoon) of bicarbonate of soda in 500 ml (1 pint) of warm water makes a soothing eyebath for itchy eyes.

Slices of cucumber placed over the eyes relieves puffiness.

Eye compresses, in the form of used/dampened herbal teabags cooled in the fridge or pads fashioned out of lint bandages and soaked in a decoction of your preferred therapeutic herb, also work wonders. To make a decoction, place 25 g (1 oz) of the fresh herb (or half that amount if you're using dried herbs), chopped up if necessary, into a saucepan (but not an aluminium or copper one), add 500 (1 pint) of distilled water (or mineral water) and bring the water to the boil. Simmer for thirty minutes to reduce the liquid by half (if more has evaporated, top up the liquid to 250 ml (1/2 pint) with water), then remove the saucepan from the heat and leave the mixture to cool. Strain the decoction through a coffee-filter paper two or three times, transfer it to a bottle and keep it in the fridge (it should be used within a few days). To soothe your eyes, soak two lint-bandage pads in the solution, lie down, place the pads over your eyes and enjoy a rest. Alternatively, if you freeze the decoction in an ice-cube tray, you'll be able to rub a therapeutic cube around your eyes and over your eyelids whenever you feel the need.

Herbs for eyes

- calendula soothes sore eyes;
- camomile revives tired eyes;
- fennel seeds add sparkle;
- mint banishes dark circles under the eyes.

YOUR CROWNING GLORY

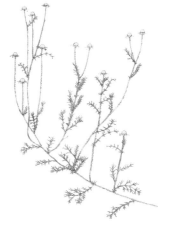

Certain herbs have long been taken for their therapeutic benefits.

What you eat, and your lifestyle, is reflected in your hair: stress, hormonal activity, lack of sleep, too much sun, swimming in chlorinated pools or salty seas, the hardness or softness of your tap water, along with any chemical hair rinses or treatments that you use on your hair, will all have visible effects.

Nearly every shampoo on the market today seems to contain the essence of fruits, flowers or herbs. In such commercial products, the much-vaunted 'natural' ingredient is, however, likely to be a chemically synthesised version, so why not use the real thing instead? Make your own herbal shampoo by pouring one application of baby shampoo into a cup, adding four drops of an essential oil, mixing the ingredients thoroughly and then using the enriched shampoo in the normal way. For dry hair, try essential oil of sage; for greasy hair, lavender or peppermint; while to prevent dandruff, use camomile, rosemary or thyme.

A few drops of essential oils in baby shampoo makes a wonderful hair treatment.

If you'd prefer to stick to commercial shampoos, try out different products until you find the one that suits you best, but don't be surprised when it stops working as well as it once did and just change to another because your hair may be crying out for a change. Wash your hair whenever it starts to look dull or greasy – wash it every day if you need to, but use a mild, gentle shampoo like baby shampoo. (In generally, shampoos that produce the least lather are the gentlest.)

If you can't wash your hair for whatever reason, don't despair because there are some easy ways of cleaning and reviving it until you can.

- Sprinkle cornflour or baby shampoo over your hair and then brush it out thoroughly. Both of these treatments are as effective as any commercial dry-shampoo product.

- Dip a number of 10 cm (4 in) squares of muslin or fine gauze in rose water, orange water or, for greasy hair, lavender water. Force the muslin over the bristles of your hairbrush and then stroke through your hair, working in sections. Repeat this process using fresh muslin squares until they pick up no more dirt.

- If you've very little time to spare, apply a little eau de cologne to a cotton-wool ball and gently swab your scalp with it. You'll feel instantly revived, and your hair will smell wonderful, too.

HAIR TREATMENTS AND CONDITIONERS

Whatever your hair type, there's a treatment to enhance it.

Protein treatment

This treatment will revive hair with damaged ends, dried-out and sun- or bleach-damaged hair. Simply whisk together three whole eggs and 15 ml (1 tablespoon) of lemon juice or cider vinegar, apply the mixture to clean, damp hair and leave it on for fifteen minutes before rinsing it off with cool water.

Fresh eggs make a good protein hair treatment.

Cider vinegar

A tonic for greasy hair, cider vinegar counteracts shampoo's alkalinity, helping to maintain the hair's correct pH balance. It also makes hair wonderfully shiny and manageable. Just add a generous dash of cider vinegar to the final rinsing water.

ROSEMARY RINSE

A rosemary rinse is a treat for normal hair. To make it, place three or four sprigs of rosemary, each about as long as your finger, in a jug, pour over boiling water and leave the infusion to steep for one hour. Then strain the liquid and use it as the final rinsing water.

Top tonsorial tip

If the water that you use for your final rinse is cool rather than warm, it will encourage each hair's outer cells to lie flat, giving your hair a smooth, shiny finish.

Oil treatments

To give it a deep-conditioning treatment, treat your hair to an oil massage, leaving the oil on your hair for as long as possible before shampooing it off.

Coconut and olive oil have long been used to condition and add luster to hair, and you can also make your own herbal hair oil by adding six drops of one of the essential oils recommended for your hair type (see page179) to 30 ml (2 tablespoons) of almond or sunflower oil. Warm the oil gently by placing a little in a bowl over a saucepan of hot water, then pour a little into the palm of your hand and rub both of your hands together before massaging the oil thoroughly into your scalp and through your hair. Repeat this process until all of the oil has been used up. Now soak a towel in hot water and wring it out, wrap your head in some kitchen foil, put on a shower cap and wrap the hot towel around it. Try to leave the oil on your head for at least thirty minutes, and when it becomes cool, replace the towel with another hot, damp one. After your time's up, wash off the oil with a mild shampoo.

Colour treatments

Camomile has been used to lighten fair hair for many centuries. To lighten blonde hair gradually over the weeks without any harsh consequences, boil 1 tablespoon of dried, or a handful of fresh camomile, or a camomile herbal teabag, in 250 ml (1/2 pint) of water, add the juice of half a lemon and then leave the decoction to cool before adding it to the final rinsing water.

To darken hair, and to disguise grey hairs, make a decoction as described above to add to the final rinsing water, but use sage and rosemary leaves rather than camomile.

Henna has long been used to give hair a reddish tint, and if this is the effect that you're after, try making a decoction (described above) of saffron to add to the final rinsing water.

Cuts, combs and brushes

Having your hair trimmed every six to eight weeks will keep it in good condition, remove damaged ends and maintain its style. If you are growing your hair, don't stop having it trimmed, just ask for the minimum amount to be snipped off. It is said that if you have to comb your hair more than three times a day to keep it in style, it's time to have it cut.

On the subject of combs, use a wide-toothed comb for disentangling windswept or wet hair and avoid brushes with densely packed bristles, which can pull and stretch your hair. If you use a pure-bristle brush, you'll need to keep the bristles in perfect condition. To do this, clean bristle brushes in a solution of warm water, a walnut-sized piece of washing soda and a few drops of ammonia. Tap the bristles very gently up and down in the solution, but without wetting the base, then rinse them in clean water in the same way and leave them to dry naturally, facing downwards, away from direct heat.

CARING FOR YOUR TEETH

Most commercial toothpastes contain abrasives, detergents, sweeteners and optical brighteners, but some everyday – and often more natural – household products and ingredients work just as effectively.

- A sage leaf rubbed over your teeth and gums is an effective cleaner and polisher.
- A paste made of 5 ml (1 teaspoon) of bicarbonate of soda, two drops of essential oil of peppermint and a little water makes an excellent toothpaste.
- If you're a heavy tea- or coffee-drinker – or smoker – rather than buying a harsh, abrasive, proprietary toothpowder, rub either a strawberry over your teeth or the wet side of a piece of lemon peel.

Nothing discolours teeth like tea or coffee, but help is at hand.

- Fresh parsley or watercress, which are both high in chlorophyll (the main ingredient in most commercial mouthwashes), are effective breath-fresheners when chewed.
- Chewing a cardamom seed in its husk is the best antidote to garlicky breath; when the husk has become soft, throw it away and swallow the seed. The next most effective cure – if you can stand it – is to chew and swallow half a lemon, skin and all! A coffee bean or parsley are also effective at temporarily masking breath odours.
- For temporary relief of toothache until you can see the dentist, apply a drop of oil of cloves to the problem tooth.
- Finally, don't forget to pamper your lips. The most effective – and cheapest – lip balm is petroleum jelly, which you could mix with the last bit of lipstick in the cylinder to make a tinted lip gloss.

Make sure you change your toothbrush regularly – but keep old ones for cleaning around the house!

HANDS AND FEET

We all too often neglect those hard-working and long-suffering parts of our bodies: our hands and feet. Our hands are constantly being subjected to extreme variations in temperature, are exposed to chemicals and plunged into harsh detergents, while our feet spend most of their day encased in shoes that, for sartorial reasons, have little in common with the anatomy of the foot.

Spare a thought for what our feet have to endure each day, and give them the attention they deserve.

Although hand cream is the best-known treatment for hands, the trouble is that as soon as you put it on, it feels so greasy that you want to wash it off again, which is partly why the best time to treat your hands is at bedtime. Buy a pair of white cotton gloves and at bedtime smother your hands in hand cream, put on your cotton gloves and let your hands soak up their well-deserved treatment while you sleep. You can do the same for your feet by covering them in a pair of loose-fitting white cotton socks. The following treatments are suitable for both hands and feet.

- When soap has failed to shift the dirt on your hands or feet, rub in some petroleum jelly, leave it on for five minutes and then wash it off with soap and warm water.

- To soothe dry and hard-working hands, rub in a drop or two of neat glycerine every night.

- For rough hands, pour a little vegetable oil – sunflower, almond and olive oil are all excellent – into your cupped palm and then add the same amount of granulated sugar (the sugar granules will rub off the rough bits of skin). Now rub your hands together vigorously for five minutes, making sure that you work the mixture over all of the skin, and then rinse your hands before letting them dry naturally.

You can clean stained hands by rubbing them with the cut surface of half a lemon. Cigarette stains need something a little stronger, however: dab on some 20 volume hydrogen peroxide and then rinse it off thoroughly. Now spare a thought for what the cigarettes are doing to your lungs!

Foot baths and other treatments

The traditional foot bath remains the best therapy for feet after a hard day.

- To revitalise tired feet, add a generous handful of fresh sage, bay, lavender or thyme (or a couple of tablespoons of the dried herb), along with 15 ml (1 tablespoon) of sea salt, to a bowl of hot water. Allow the water to cool as you soak your feet.

Lavender in dried form or as an essential oil lifts body and spirit.

- To alleviate itchy feet, add 60 ml (4 tablespoons) of cider vinegar to your foot bath.
- To revive cold feet – or treat a head cold – soak your feet in a foot bath to which you've added a couple of teaspoons of mustard powder.
- Seaweed is a wonderful soother of aching feet, so remember to bring some back with you the next time you go on seaside holiday!
- To treat smelly feet, add lots of sage to your foot bath.

The main reason why feet become smelly is because your hosiery and shoes are restricting the flow of air around your feet, which means that the sweat can't evaporate. Trying these tips may help to solve the problem.

- Wash your feet several times a day – or as frequently as possible – and then dry them thoroughly.

Walking barefoot on the beach or through grass is one of the best treats you can give your feet.

Don't wear socks or other types of hosiery that contain synthetic fibres or shoes that have synthetic linings.

- Go barefoot as often as you can. Walking barefoot along the beach or on soft grass is both physically and mentally beneficial.
- Before putting on footwear, dust your feet, and especially between your toes, with foot powder. Dabbing surgical spirit onto your feet in the morning and at night may also help.
- Let your shoes dry out after you've taken them off, and don't wear the same pair of shoes for two days in a row.
- Sprinkle the insides of your shoes with a teaspoon of bicarbonate of soda (baking soda), shake each shoe to spread the powder around and then leave them in the open air for a couple of hours.

Finger- and toenails

All of the old advice about not filing your nails using a to-and-fro motion, not cutting your fingernails with scissors and cutting your toenails straight across is absolutely true. Not only will nails split more easily if you rub a nail file back and forth over them, but they prefer to be filed with emery boards rather than metal nail files.

Keeping your nails clean and well cared for can be tricky, so here are some tips to help you to keep on top of the task.

- If you are about to do a dirty job like gardening or cleaning, try putting a dollop of lanolin or petroleum jelly under each nail before you begin.
- Treat your feet to a weekly pedicure. The best time to do this is after a bath, when the skin on your feet is warm, soft and clean. Make sure that your feet are dry before starting, and take your time (a ballerina once told me that she had to miss several performances because she had rushed her pedicure and had cut her nails badly).

- Cuticles need particular attention: never force back overgrown cuticles, but instead regularly rub in a little petroleum jelly, which will eventually make them soft enough to push back with a cotton-wool bud.
- The old way of adding shine to nails was to buff them with nail powder and a chamois-leather buffer, and this is still a good way to improve the appearance of your nails if you don't want to use a coloured nail varnish. Whiting – a pure, white chalk that has been ground and washed – makes an excellent nail powder. Remember that you should buff your nails in one direction only rather than backwards and forwards to avoid causing them to heat up, dry out and then split.
- Nail varnish will last longer if you rub your thumb around the edge of the nail while it's still wet because doing this will remove any minute 'overhangs' that can catch on things and thus cause chips in your nail varnish.
- Your nails will look longer if you don't take nail varnish to their outer edges.
- If you run out of nail-varnish remover, use acetone, surgical spirit or even some left-over perfume instead. Remember to wash your nails thoroughly afterwards and then to rub a little olive or almond oil or petroleum jelly into them.

FINISHING TOUCHES

Some final tips will give your finishing touches more impact.

- Keep your perfume in a cool, dark place to avoid exposure to air and light.
- If you want your perfume to last a little longer after you've put it on, before applying it, rub a tiny bit of petroleum jelly into your skin.

The finishing touch: a favourite perfume completes a beauty routine.

- Buying a higher concentration of your favourite perfume will ensure that it lasts longer. An extrait or parfum contains between 15 and 30 per cent pure perfume essence; parfum de toilette or eau de parfum is less concentrated at between 8 and 15 per cent, while the lightest concentrations are eau de toilette (between 4 and 8 per cent), eau de cologne (between 3 and 5 per cent) and splash-on cologne (between 1and 3%).

- Because a perfume's scent rises, the best places on your body to apply it are behind your knees and on your ankles. Pulse points, where the blood runs close to the skin, making it warmer and thus encouraging the scent to develop, are also good, so apply it behind your ears, on the nape of your neck, on the insides of your wrists (although it does get washed off easily here), on your temples and in the crooks of your elbows.

- Before using them, chill eyebrow pencils and lip-liners in the freezer for a few minutes to prevent them from breaking or smudging because they are too soft.

- If your mascara has dried in its tube, if you screw the top on tightly and immerse the base in hot water, you should be able to salvage enough for one application.

- To make your eyelashes look longer, brush your lashes towards the outer edge of your eyes when applying mascara.

HOME MAINTENANCE

K eeping your home in good condition will not only help to maintain its value, but can add significantly to it, while decorating gives you the opportunity to express your likes and personality through colour, texture and pattern. You can also save a great deal of money by 'doing it yourself', although you must be prepared to spend a significant amount of your free time on a task in order to complete

it. A little basic know-how regarding how things work, why they go wrong and how to put things right – even if it's only for a short time until you can call in a professional – can save you time, money and tears!

The first rule of any DIY project is to think carefully before you start. Do you have the right tools and enough experience to complete the job to a satisfactory and safe level? Do you have the time and energy to do it all yourself? Are you legally allowed to do it? Some of the more complex types of household maintenance and improvement (such as gas and gas-appliance installation) require high levels of professional skill and only those who are legally licensed by a

Think before you start: DIY depends on good planning.

relevant professional body or association are qualified and permitted to do it. Furthermore, if you live in rented accommodation or are the leaseholder of your home, your landlord or freeholder may be required to give their consent to any changes. You will also need to consider your neighbours and before starting work should inform them of any noise or other type of disturbance that may occur. And don't forget that you'll have to get rid of incidental rubbish afterwards: empty paint tins, dirty paint-stripper and cleaning solutions, old plaster, stripped-off wallpaper and all of the other detritus of even a single room's redecoration will need to be disposed of. Don't expect your regular household-refuse collection service team to deal with it either, and remember that in many cases, such waste needs disposing of carefully and safely, especially if there are chemicals involved. Contact your local council for advice on waste disposal – and any charges for collection – before starting work.

Make sure you have – and wear – protective clothing when required.

The second rule of any DIY project is to be safe. Don't tackle any job – however small – if you don't feel confident, and where gas and electricity are concerned, always call in a professional. Always read the labels on products, and because most paints and solvents contain harmful chemicals, you'd be well advised to wear protective clothing, such as gloves or eye-protectors, as directed; a face mask will also be required when fumes or dust may be a hazard. Make sure that you use the right equipment: don't try to gain access to hard-to-reach areas by standing on a chair, for example, and instead use a ladder, ensure that it is stable and never over-reach yourself, but rather get down from the ladder and move it to a new position so that you can reach your target with ease. Before working around electrical fittings, such as switches and sockets – especially when there is wet paint or wallpaper paste in the vicinity, increasing the danger of an electrical shock – isolate their fuses in the main consumer unit (fuse box) to shut off the power flowing to them.

The third rule of any DIY project is that the results will only be as good as the preparation. No amount of expensive new wallpaper is going to look wonderful if the walls underneath are bumpy, lumpy, uneven or full of holes. A newly painted room won't look so impressive if the floors, windows and light switches are covered in paint dribbles. And if you have to replace a ruined carpet because you couldn't be bothered to take it up or cover it before you started decorating, all the money that you saved 'doing it yourself' will have been wasted.

The finished look is only as good as the preparation: take time to prepare surfaces by sanding, planning and cleaning them first.

HOME DECORATING

The huge interest in home decoration has been fuelled by books telling you how to create special effects like crackle-glazed, rag-rolled, faux-marbled and distressed looks, as well as by countless television home makeover programmes. An industry has been created that offers a vast range of different decorating materials in an enormous spectrum of colours, all designed for the DIY market. What were once the closely guarded secrets of interior designers and professional painters and decorators have now been revealed to the amateur enthusiast.

Which paint to use?

Despite the huge ranges that you'll find in DIY superstores, there are, in fact, really only two main types of house paint: water-based and solvent-based paint (which is sometimes, albeit inaccurately, called 'oil-based paint').

Water-based paints include emulsion, quick-drying eggshell and water-based gloss. These are ideal for walls, while the gloss can be used on most interior woodwork. Modern emulsions normally contain vinyl, which makes them both durable and easy to clean, and are available in a variety of finishes, from matt through silk to soft sheen, as well as textured finishes.

Look carefully at the range of paints available to select the finish you want.

Solvent-based paints include traditional eggshell and gloss, specialist sheen finishes, lacquers and paints for metal. These are designed for areas of hard wear, for exterior and interior woodwork and metalwork. Because solvent-based paints are flammable, they must be stored carefully and according to the manufacturer's instructions. Their fumes are unpleasant, and care should therefore be taken to work in well-ventilated areas when using them.

You can determine if a paint is water- or solvent-based by reading the label on its tin: if the instructions for thinning the paint indicate that water should be used, then the paint is itself water-

Whenever possible, buy the best quality paints and brushes. These will give the best finish and will last longer.

based. Alternatively, if the thinner required is white spirit, then it is a solvent-based paint. (You will also need whichever of these substances is appropriate to clean your brushes or rollers.)

For the best results, use the same brand of primer, undercoat and topcoat for the job – they were, after all, designed and manufactured to work together!

Keep tools and equipment clean: left over paint from a previous job will spoil a finish.

Paints for special purposes

There are also certain paints that fulfil special purposes.

- Anti-condensation paints, which are especially designed for use in kitchens and bathrooms, insulate the walls, reducing the contrasts in temperatures that can cause condensation. They sometimes contain glass particles and generally a fungicide, too, to prevent mould from developing.

- Despite their slightly misleading names, anti-damp and anti-stain paints do not prevent or cure damp and stains, but instead create a synthetic barrier that renders any damp marks or stains invisible.

- Enamel paints, which are available in smooth and hammered finishes, are highly durable. Being corrosion-resistant, they can be used on bare metal, but if you intend to paint over metal that has already been painted, you will need to use a proprietary metal-primer. As well as white radiator enamel, you can buy coloured, heat-resistant enamels for cookers and fireplaces.

- Tile paint is designed to be painted over ceramic tiles, enabling you quickly to update the look of old ones, while melamine paint is ideal for restyling old melamine furniture and kitchen cabinets. In both instances, careful preparation and priming will be required.

How much paint to use?

Different types of paint cover different areas, the coverage varying according to the brand of paint and the absorbency of the surface that you are decorating. The details on the paint tin's label will guide you, but to ensure that you buy enough paint to be able to complete your task, you will first need to measure the area that you intend to paint.

Read label instructions carefully to help you work out how much you will need to cover your walls.

For walls, measure the length of the walls and then add together three of the measurements (not adding one of the shortest walls to your total allows for doors and windows). Then multiply this figure by the height of the room. For example, a room that measures 18 ft x 16 ft and that has a height of 10 ft would be:

- 2 x 18 = 36, 1 x 16 =16; 36 + 16 = 52;
- 52 x 10 = 520 sq ft
- To convert the measurement from imperial to metric, multiply 520 by 0.093, which equals 48.36 sq m.
- For a sloping ceiling, multiply the length by the width.
- For a window or door, multiply the height by the width.

Which colours to use?

- 'Warm' colours, such as red, yellow and orange, appear to bring surfaces closer. They are ideal for cool, north- or east-facing rooms, rooms with high ceilings – especially if you take the paint down to picture-rail level – and for the end wall of a long corridor or passage.

Warm colours: make a cold room feel cosy, and a high ceiling look lower.

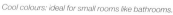
Cool colours: ideal for small rooms like bathrooms.

- 'Cool' colours, such as blue, lilac, mauve and green, make surfaces look more distant. They are suited to warm, south- or west-facing rooms and small rooms like bathrooms.
- You can also modify the effects of warm and cool colours by changing the depth of colour. Note that darker shades, which absorb more light, seem to advance towards you, while pastel shades, which reflect the light, appear more distant.
- You can disguise any unlovely features, such as cupboards, built-in wardrobes, plumbing pipework and radiators, by painting them the same colour as the background walls. Alternatively, make features of the features by painting them a contrasting colour.

Colour is affected by light, so look at paint samples in daylight and under artificial light. Note that because reflected lights are softer than central ceiling lights, you can position table or small lamps and spotlights so that they bounce light off ceilings or walls. Remember that different light sources have different effects on colour:

- ordinary tungsten light bulbs emphasise red tones, but make blues and greens look more yellow than they do in daylight;
- fluorescent lights reduce shadows and emphasise blues;
- halogen lights give out a bright, white light than can make colours look more harsh than they do in daylight.

Colour in rooms will be affected by natural and artifical light. Different lightbulbs will create different effects – and vary in economy – so choose carefully.

Preparing to paint

Good preparation is essential for a good result because neither paint nor wallpaper will adhere properly to flaking surfaces and any flaws will be magnified rather than disguised.

- Plan to spend two-thirds of your time preparing the surfaces and the final third actually painting them.
- Clear the area of as much furniture and as many furnishings as possible and cover anything that can't be removed with dustsheets. Cover door handles with kitchen foil or a plastic bag and mask off light switches with low-tack masking tape to avoid painting them as well.
- Keep pets well away from paints and newly painted surfaces. Not only can the fumes upset them, but they will inevitably end up with paint-flecked paws and tails and will also leave traces of their fur or hairs in your paintwork.
- The only way to guarantee that you won't spread paint across the floors throughout your home is to wear an old pair of shoes while painting and then to take them off and leave them by the door inside the room that you are working in before leaving it.
- If the walls are in good condition, wash them with a mild detergent solution and then rinse them before leaving them to dry. Wash the walls from the bottom upwards and make sure that you wash each wall in one go – don't abandon it to answer the phone or the doorbell otherwise you'll leave a dirty tidemark that will be nearly impossible to remove and difficult to disguise.

Avoid accidental splashes and spills by covering floors and fittings with dust sheets.

- If the walls are damp, you'll need to deal with the cause of the problem before decorating because it's simply not worth painting or wallpapering over damp marks when the source remains. To identify the cause of the damp, tape a piece of kitchen foil over a damp patch and leave it for a week. If the outer side of the foil is then wet, the problem is most likely being caused by condensation. If, on the other hand, the foil is wet on the underside, the cause is either rising damp (caused by a faulty damp-proof course) or penetrating damp (caused by moisture penetration from the outside due to faulty pointing, a badly fitting window or door or a missing or loose tile or slate on the roof).

- Once you have resolved the damp problem, first wash away any mould with a mild solution of 1 part household bleach to 4 parts water, then leave the solution on the wall for four days before rinsing it off and allowing the wall to dry.

- The next step is to remove any patches of flaking plaster, to fill any dents or holes made by nails and screws and then to sand down your repairs when they have dried so that they are flush with the wall surface. Fill any cracks and holes with flexible filler, leave it to dry and then sand it flush with the surround.

- A keyed surface provides a stable surface for new paint to adhere to, so the next task is to sand any woodwork and lightly sand walls that have been previously painted with an eggshell or solvent-based paint. If the paintwork on woodwork is sound, sand the surface lightly to key it and then wipe over it with a cloth dampened in a little white spirit to remove any grease. If there is any blistered or flaking paint on woodwork, scrape it away and then sand it down so that it is level with the surround.

Knots in wood will keep oozing resin which will spoil a paint finish, so seal knots first with a proprietary knotting solution.

- Prime all new and bare wood before painting it to seal the surface. Because the knots in new wood will continue to ooze sap, which can leach through, staining and discolouring any paint covering it, apply a knotting solution to them.
- Finally, apply a stabilising solution to powdery plaster and a plaster-primer to new plaster and then leave them to dry.

Preparing paint

Whether the paint that you are using has been newly purchased or was left over from a previous job, it's important always to follow some basic rules.

- Wipe the top and sides of the paint tin with a damp cloth to remove any dust and dirt that could otherwise contaminate the paint when you open the lid.
- Prise off the lid with the side of a knife blade or a special opener for paint tins.
- Stir liquid paint with a flat, clean, wooden stick, making sure that it reaches right down to the bottom of the tin. Doing this will ensure that the pigment and medium are thoroughly blended.
- If a skin has formed on the surface of the paint, carefully cut around it with a knife and then lift it out in one piece with a clean stick. The next time you put away a tin of paint, store it upside down, standing its lid, so that if a skin does then form, it'll be spread across the bottom of the tin when you open it.

Don't use a screwdriver because there's a danger that it will buckle the lid, which means that the lid won't provide an airtight seal when it's replaced.

- Professional decorators never dip their brushes into open tins of paint. Whether the paint is old or new, always transfer a small amount to a little bucket (what decorators call a 'kettle') and dip your brush into that. To keep the paint kettle clean, thereby ensuring that any old paint doesn't contaminate a new colour, line it with kitchen foil and when you've finished with one batch of paint, simply remove the foil, throw it away and reline the paint kettle with a new sheet.

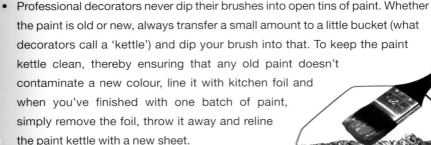

- Tying a piece of string across the top of your paint kettle will enable you to wipe any excess paint on your brush across the string rather than on the side of the kettle, thereby causing it to dribble down the outside.

Lining a paint kettle with kitchen foil makes for easy disposal and less cleaning up!

- Old tins of paint may still be perfectly usable, but make sure that the paint contains no lumps or particles of dirt, grit or dust that could spoil your finish by straining it into a paint kettle through a piece of muslin (or old pair of nylon tights) stretched over the rim.

Paint applicators

You have the choice of three types of paint applicator: rollers, brushes and pads.

Rollers

- Rollers, which can be used with both solvent and water-based paints, apply paint much faster than brushes and are best used for covering large areas. They are available in a wide variety of sizes and textures to suit different purposes: use a long-pile roller for heavily textured effects, for example, and a medium-length pile for lightly textured or smooth walls.

- Prepare new rollers by soaking them in warm, soapy water for a few hours before use to release any loose fibres that could spoil a finish. Rinse and dry them thoroughly before using them.
- You will need to load a roller from a special paint tray. Lightly dip the roller into the paint reservoir and then roll it gently over the tray's ribbed part to coat it evenly.
- When painting with a roller, use zigzag strokes so that you cover the surface from all angles.
- To avoid spraying paint all over the floor and adjacent surfaces, don't let the roller spin at the end of a stroke.
- Attach an extension handle to the roller handle to enable you to reach ceilings and the tops of walls.
- Before painting walls or ceilings with a roller, first use a small paintbrush to cut in at the corners and edges because the edge of the roller won't reach into such small spaces fully.

Paintbrushes

There are many things to bear in mind if you prefer to use paintbrushes.

- Choose a good-quality brush with which to paint walls and ceilings because cheap brushes tend to shed their bristles.
- A brush that is about 20 cm (roughly 8 in) wide gives the quickest coverage,

Use the right brush for the job. Look after equipment, and it will last longer.

but if you are not used to painting, your wrist will soon tire when using it. Although the job may take a little longer to complete, you may find a brush that is 15 cm (about 6 in) wide, along with one that is 5 cm (about 2 in) wide to use when cutting in at the edges, more comfortable to use.

Rub the bristles of newly purchased brushes in the palm of your hand to remove any loose dust and bristles.

- Soaking new paintbrushes in linseed oil for twenty-four hours before use will make them both easier to work with and easier to clean. Remember to remove the oil with white spirit before starting to paint.
- Although professional decorators hold their brushes like pens, the important thing is to hold the brush in the way that you find the most comfortable.
- When painting walls with a brush, start at a top corner. If you are right-handed, work from right to left.
- Paint an area measuring about 20 sq cm (2 sq ft) at a time. If you're using emulsion paint, paint in horizontal bands, but if you're using solvent-based paint, painting in vertical strips means that the junctions are less likely to show (that is, unless you blend in the wet edges quickly).
- Always finish painting a wall before taking a break or you may find that there is a visible change of tone in areas that have been painted at different times.
- Keep a set of brushes (or pads and a roller) for use with white paint only because no matter how thoroughly brushes are cleaned, remnants of a coloured paint that was previously used will otherwise always end up being deposited on newly painted white paintwork.

Dip only the first third of the brush into paint. Overloading a brush causes paint dribbles, while if paint is allowed to run into the base of the brush, the bristles will be ruined.

Paint pads

- Paint pads are designed to apply paint to large, flat surfaces and are supplied with their own special paint trays. Their rectangular faces, which are covered with short, mohair fibres, are backed with plastic foam, which ensures that the pad is always in contact with a wall's surface, even if it is rough.

- To apply the paint, first load the pad by drawing it across the paint tray and then sweep the pad gently and evenly against the wall. Although you can generally move the pad in any direction, when working with emulsion paints, use crisscrossing strokes, while when using solvent-based paints, finish with vertical strokes to avoid leaving streaks.

The order of painting

- Rooms should be painted from top to bottom, starting with the ceiling, then the walls, doors and window frames and lastly the skirting boards.

Painting ceilings

- To paint a ceiling – which can be very hard work – start by cutting in around the edge of the ceiling (where it meets the walls) with a small brush. Next, paint a wider strip parallel to one edge with a wide brush, roller or pad, leaving a small gap. When you come to the end of one run – one strip of painted ceiling – reverse the direction and fill the gap. Recharge your brush, roller or pad with more paint and then start a new run, again leaving a small gap, and continue to paint the ceiling in this way.

Painting doors and window frames

- You'll find it a lot easier to paint a door if you take it off its hinges and lay it flat across a couple of trestles or strong supports. Remove any door furniture, such as handles, escutcheons and finger plates, if possible, too, or else mask such items off to ward against getting paint on them.

- Paint the components of a panelled door in the following order: the mouldings (if there are any); the small panels inside the mouldings; the vertical strip running down the centre of the door; the horizontal strips at the top and bottom and in the middle of the door; and finally, the two outer vertical strips, followed by the edges and the frame. When painting the edges of a door, be sure to wedge the door open to stop paint from sticking to the frame as it dries, and if it is painted in a different colour, mask off the edges of the other side of the door, too.

- Before painting window frames, apply low-tack masking tape around the edges of the glass, but leave a gap of about 1 mm (1/32 in) between the masking tape and window frame because applying paint here will form a protective seal.

- To paint casement windows (those that open sideways), first paint the glazing bars (if there are any) and then paint the rest of the window, apart from the outside edge, which should match the exterior paintwork. Finish by painting the window frame and sill.

- To paint sash windows (those that slide up and down), open the window so that the bottom and top sashes overlap by about 20 cm (8 in). Paint the bottom of the top sash; close the bottom sash and pull up the top one until it is almost closed; paint the rest of the top sash; paint the bottom sash; and, finally, paint the frame, taking care not to apply paint to the sash cords.

Painting skirting boards and picture rails

- When painting such woodwork as skirting boards and picture rails, take your brush along the grain of the wood. On wide surfaces, apply the paint in long,

narrow, horizontal bands. When painting the second band, work your brush across the grain to join this strip with the previous one and then 'lay off' (paint using very light strokes) along the grain to remove any brushstrokes and achieve a smooth finish.

Cleaning and storing your tools

Looking after your tools and materials properly will prolong their lives, so observe the following tips.

- Note that brushes should be cleaned at the end of each painting day and should not be left standing in a jar of solvent for several days.
- Either wipe excess paint from tools with newspaper or remove it from rollers by running them over sheets of newspaper.

- Clean brushes, rollers and pads that have been used with water-based paints by suspending them in a warm solution of soap and water for a few minutes. Do not immerse any wooden handles, however, because this will cause them to swell and eventually split.

Wipe off excess paint at the end of a job on old newspapers.

If you need to take a short break between painting sessions, wrap any brushes, rollers or pads that you've been using in clingfilm, a plastic bag or kitchen foil to prevent them from drying out.

- Clean brushes that have been used with solvent-based paints by suspending them in a jar of white spirit or proprietary brush-cleaner. Rather than risking the bristles being squashed against the bottom of the jar, drill a hole through the brush handle, insert a long nail through the hole and balance the ends of the nail on the rim of the jar. Finish by cleaning the brush with soap and water.
- Remove any stubborn paint marks from tools with a nailbrush.
- After you've cleaned your brushes, rinse them in cool water and then apply a dollop of hair or fabric conditioner to the bristles to keep them in top condition.
- Suspend brushes, rollers and pads by their handles before leaving them to dry.
- Work a few drops of cooking, baby or linseed oil into the bristles of clean, dry brushes to keep them soft until the brushes are used again.
- If you aren't going to use them for a while, prevent mildew from developing by either storing brushes in a dust-free, well-ventilated place or wrapping them in newspaper and securing it with a rubber band.
- If you find that the bristles of a paintbrush have become stiff, simmer the brush in vinegar until they have become soft and then scrape off the old paint with a nailbrush or wire brush. Wash the bristles in soapy water before rinsing and conditioning them and leaving them to dry.
- Smearing a little petroleum jelly around the rim of a paint tin before replacing its lids will help to maintain an airtight seal.

Reseal a paint tin by placing a stout piece of wood over the lid and hitting it with a hammer as you move it around the rim to ensure that the lid is evenly secured.

- Once sealed firmly, store paint tins upside down to prevent a skin from forming on the surface.
- Dab a little of the paint that it contains on the base of the paint tin so that you can instantly identify its colour.
- Rubbing ordinary vegetable oil into your hands will remove any paint that has dried on your skin more gently than a chemical solvent like turpentine or white spirit.
- Reduce the lingering smell of paint by placing half an onion, cut side facing downwards on a plate, in the room being decorated. The onion will absorb much of the odour and should be replaced daily until the smell of paint has disappeared.

Common paint problems and how to solve them

Sometimes the paint effect achieved is not what you intended. Here are the solutions to some common paint problems.

Drips and dribbles

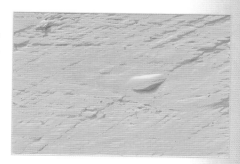

- Drips and dribbles, which are commonly caused by overloading the paintbrush with paint, befall even professional decorators. Once the paint has dried, sand down the drips and dribbles and repaint the area.

Sagging paint

- Sagging paint is manifested as obvious streaks of paint, most often in gloss paint, caused by an overloaded paintbrush or not spreading out the paint enough. Allow several days for the paint to dry, then rub it down with a fine-grade abrasive sandpaper.

Cissing

- The 'see-through' effect of cissing usually occurs when you've tried to paint an emulsion over a gloss paint. It can also happen if you don't stir the paint enough, if the paint is too thin or if you've used the wrong undercoat. Wait until the paint is completely dry, then sand it down and apply another topcoat.

VISIBLE BRUSHSTROKES

- Visible brushstrokes are normally caused by poor-quality brushes or overly thick paint. Once the paint has dried, sand down the brushstrokes and repaint the area.

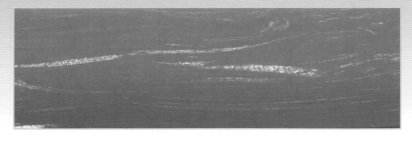

Cracking and flaking paint

- When emulsion paint cracks and flakes, it usually means that dust has been trapped under it. In the case of solvent-based paints, cracking or flaking is usually caused by underlying moisture: either damp or a first coat that was not completely dry. In both cases you'll need to strip off the paint completely, clean, prime and then repaint the area. A flaking surface sometimes indicates that there is rotten wood underneath; test it by poking the wood with a sharp point, and if the point penetrates the wood easily, the wood is rotten and should be replaced. If the wood is sound, however, you'll again need to strip off the paint, clean, prime and repaint the wood.

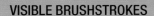

Pimply paint

- Small pimples on the surface of areas of paint indicate that specks of dust or dirt have been trapped beneath the paint. Either you didn't spend enough time preparing the surface or your brush picked up dust and dirt as you worked (possibly from the floor if the pimples are on the skirting board). Lightly sand down the surface, wipe it with a damp cloth and then repaint the area.

WALLPAPER

- Wallpapering is the quickest way of adding colour and texture to a room. If you are not sure which colour or pattern you want, take a small fabric sample from a curtain or carpet in the room when going wallpaper shopping to help you to find the right match. Once you've found a wallpaper that you like, check that it won't be discontinued in the near future so that you can buy more if you decide to use the same paper in another room.

Add colour, pattern and texture to a room with wallpaper.

- Lining paper is a cheap, buff-coloured wallpaper that is used for lining uneven or impervious walls prior to hanging wallpaper. (Although most wall-coverings will hide or disguise minor blemishes, the walls should still be as clean and smooth as possible before lining paper is hung.) Lining a wall will ensure a professional finish, and you can also use lining paper to provide an even surface for emulsion paint. Unlike the wallpaper itself, which is hung in vertical strips, lining paper is hung horizontally to avoid the seams overlapping. On ceilings, hang lining paper across the width and wallpaper along the length.

- Relief papers, or 'white' papers, have deeply embossed patterns and are useful for hiding minor imperfections in walls. The best-known and cheapest relief paper is woodchip (in which particles of wood are sandwiched between two layers of paper), which is easy to hang and designed to be

Relief wallpaper has an embossed pattern and is available in a range of weights.

painted over. Other relief papers include Anaglypta (in which two pieces of paper are bonded together and embossed); Supaglypta (a stronger version of Anaglypta, which is made with cotton fibres and is capable of withstanding deeper embossing), Lincrusta (consisting of a solid layer of linseed oil and fillers fused onto backing paper and then engraved); and Vinaglypta (a deeply embossed, expanded vinyl that is designed to be painted over).

- Vinyls are durable, washable wallpapers that are suitable for kitchens and bathrooms. Most are sold ready-pasted for easy application.

- Printed papers are available in a huge range of patterns, styles and finishes, including washable papers and vinyls. Matching up the patterns on some wallpapers can be very straightforward, but you'll need a little more patience – and more paper – when matching up others. Wallpaper manufacturers print information in the form of symbols on each roll, so look out for these when shopping for wallpaper.

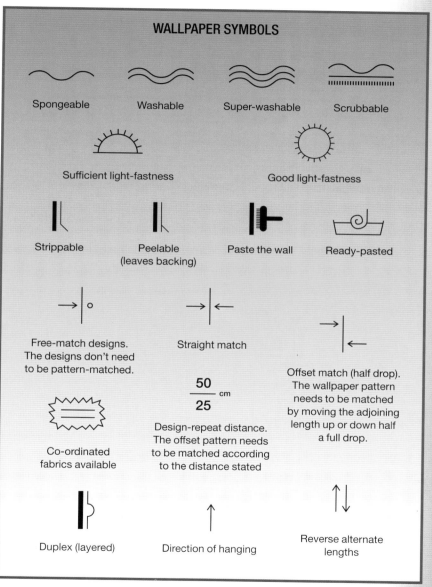

WALLPAPER SYMBOLS

Spongeable

Washable

Super-washable

Scrubbable

Sufficient light-fastness

Good light-fastness

Strippable

Peelable
(leaves backing)

Paste the wall

Ready-pasted

Free-match designs.
The designs don't need
to be pattern-matched.

Straight match

Offset match (half drop).
The wallpaper pattern
needs to be matched
by moving the adjoining
length up or down half
a full drop.

$$\frac{50}{25} \text{ cm}$$

Design-repeat distance.
The offset pattern needs
to be matched according
to the distance stated

Co-ordinated
fabrics available

Duplex (layered)

Direction of hanging

Reverse alternate
lengths

WALLPAPER DESIGN TIPS

Bear these tips in mind when choosing a wallpaper for a particular room.

Large patterns seem to reduce the size of a room.

Small patterns on a light ground make a little room look bigger.

Stripes look best on even walls and walls where a picture rail or cornice provides a break between the wall and ceiling.

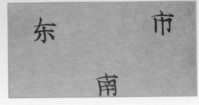

Small, random patterns help to disguise bumpy, uneven walls.

How much wallpaper to use?

A standard roll of wallpaper measures about 10 m (33 ft) in length by 53 cm (21 in) in width (although American and Continental European wallpapers may differ) and will cover about 5.4 sq m (58 sq ft).

To ascertain how many rolls of wallpaper you will need, start by measuring the height and perimeter of the room. Next, draw a simple plan showing the doors, windows and fireplace (if there is one). Use the table below to work out how many rolls you will need, then add an extra roll to be on the safe side. Most suppliers offer refunds on any unopened, unused rolls, but check first before buying your wallpaper.

To estimate the number of rolls that you will need to cover a ceiling, using metric measurements, measure the length and width of the room and multiply the two figures, then divide the result by five for the number of rolls required.

Which paste to use?

- The label on the wallpaper roll will advise you which type of paste is suitable for use.
- Cold-water paste is suitable for all types of wall and ceiling paper, apart from vinyls. You will need to mix a fresh amount of paste each day.
- Despite its name, hot-water paste needs to be cool before it is applied. It is suitable for use with all types of wallpaper except for vinyls.
- Fungicidal paste is especially good for use with vinyls because it dries more slowly than other pastes. Keep children and pets away from this paste, however, and certainly don't let them touch or taste it!
- Cellulose paste is thin, quick-drying and designed for use with lightweight wallpapers and those whose printed faces may easily become marked.
- Overlap adhesive is stronger than ordinary paste, but is only intended for use with wallpapers that are already peeling off walls.
- When mixing wallpaper paste, follow the manufacturer's instructions, use a clean stick to mix it thoroughly and then leave it to settle until all of the bubbles have subsided.
- You may find it quicker and easier to apply the paste to wallpaper using a roller rather than a brush, but whichever you use, follow the pasting-technique tips on page 214.

Using a roller instead of a brush to apply wallpaper paste can be quicker and easier.

Preparing to wallpaper

- Before hanging new wallpaper, remove any existing wallpaper. When peeling off vinyl wallpaper, start at the bottom. You'll probably find lining paper underneath, which you can either remove or leave in place and then hang your new wallpaper directly over it.

A large pasting brush will distribute paste evenly over the paper.

- Wash any previously painted surfaces and allow them to dry. Cover any grease spots (which are common on kitchen walls due to cooking splashes and hands touching the walls) with latex to prevent the grease from bleeding through your new wallpaper.
- To ensure a smooth finish, hang lining paper on the walls and leave it to dry for forty-eight hours before hanging wallpaper over the top.

Pasting techniques

- Place a measured and cut length of wallpaper on a pasting table, design side facing downwards, making sure that the paper overlaps both the edge of the table nearest to you and one end (this will prevent the paste from marking the face of the paper).
- Using a pasting brush, evenly spread paste over the back of the paper nearest to you, but not over the area whose boundary is 30 cm (12 in) away from the far edge of the table.
- Move the paper to the other side of the table and apply paste to the uncovered area.
- Fold the pasted paper over itself about two-thirds of the way down, then move the unpasted paper onto the table and cover it with paste as described above.
- Fold the bottom length of paper over itself once more and position it so that it is almost touching the top fold.

Soaking wallpapers

- All wallpapers need to be soaked for a certain amount of time to enable them to absorb the paste. Too long a soak, and the paper will tear easily and be hard to hang; too short a time, however, and the paper will come away from the wall. You will find the manufacturer's recommended soaking time on the wallpaper's label. While the first length of paper is soaking, paste a second length, and by the time that this piece is ready, the first length should be ready to hang.

Hanging: where to start?

- Start hanging wallpaper at the focal point of the room. If there is a fireplace, for example, this should be your starting point. Find the centre of the fireplace and then plumb a vertical line down the wall above it by hanging a weighted string from the top of the wall, where it joins the ceiling or the cornice. Mark the plumbed line with a pencil all of the way down the wall. Hang the first piece of wallpaper to the right of this line and then work in a clockwise direction as you hang subsequent lengths around the room.
- If there is no fireplace, however, start papering at a window, working away from the light and again in a clockwise direction.

Hanging the first length

- Take the first length of pasted wallpaper and hold the top section against the wall with one hand, lining the left edge against the pencil line on the wall. Support the rest of the folded paper with your other hand.
- Position the top edge of the wallpaper at the junction of the wall and ceiling or cornice, leaving a 5 cm (2 in) overlap to trim later.

Using a paperhanger's brush, smooth the paper firmly, but gently, into position. Work downwards, brushing the paper from top to bottom to remove any bubbles or creases.

- When you reach the bottom, don't smooth the bottom end of the paper, but instead leave it resting on the skirting board. Now return to the top.
- Run the blunt edge of a pair of scissors gently along the line in the paper between the wall and ceiling or cornice to emphasise the crease, then gently pull the wallpaper away from the wall and cut along the crease to trim off the excess before brushing the paper back onto the wall.
- Return to the bottom of the wall and trim off the excess paper in the same way as outlined above. Now wipe any excess paste off the ceiling and skirting board.
- Measure, cut, paste and hang – matching up the pattern if necessary – the second and subsequent lengths in the same way.

Working in and around corners

- Don't try to fit a complete width of wallpaper over, or into, a corner because it will only crease and tear if you do so. The best way to tackle internal and external corners is to measure the width of the wall from the last drop of paper to the corner and then to add 2.5 cm (1 in) to this figure. It is this 2.5 cm (1 in) section of paper that should be wrapped over, or into, the corner (it sometimes helps to cut a series of diagonal nicks in the very edge to encourage it to fold over, or into, the corner neatly). As you work around, or out of, the corner, the next piece of paper should be hung so that it overlaps and hides this edge. You will, however, need some overlap adhesive to ensure that the paper adheres to itself.

Wallpaper problems and solutions

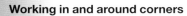

- Bubbles in wallpaper are a common problem and are often caused by too much paste having been applied, although they also can occur because too little has been used and the bubble is full of air. Don't do anything about bubbles for at least twenty-four hours because they will sometimes disappear on their own. If one then remains, however, carefully pierce it with the point of a

very sharp craft knife to enable any excess paste to escape. Now wipe down the bubble with a clean, damp sponge. If no paste emerges, it indicates that the bubble is made of air, and you'll need to fill it with a little paste applied with an artist's paintbrush and then sponge it down.

- Shiny patches on wallpaper are due to the paste drying on the surface. These can be removed by rubbing them gently with a ball of white bread.

DIY TIPS

By keeping your home in good repair, you'll be ensuring that your fixtures, fittings and equipment work properly and that any long and costly repairs are avoided. Most household repairs are simple and straightforward if you deal with them as soon as you spot that they are needed, and usually require only a little skill, some patience and, most importantly, common sense, especially where safety is concerned. If you don't feel confident enough to tackle any repair, no matter how small or insignificant it may seem, or don't have the time and energy to see it through to the end, call in a professional.

Most DIY superstores offer very useful, free, 'how to' leaflets that explain in simple steps how to do practically anything, from fixing a dripping tap to converting your loft. These are well worth collecting and keeping in a file in case of emergency: if all of the lights go out, for example, or you come home to find a flood in your kitchen or bathroom, these leaflets will help you to deal with the problem calmly and safely.

As a householder, you should be prepared for such problems as dripping taps and little leaks, which, although minor irritations, may become serious – and dangerous if they occur near electrical wiring – if left unattended. Keep your tool kit ready for action and store it in a place that you can get at easily. Perhaps the most vital piece of emergency equipment is a good torch (never try to undertake any repair by candlelight).

The basics

It's crucial that you either acquaint yourself with, or implement, some DIY basics.

- Make sure that you know where to turn off the water supply in your home. It's advisable to turn the mains stopcock on and off occasionally so that it won't be too stiff if you have to turn it off in an emergency.

- Ensure that you know how to turn off the power supply – both the electricity and gas – to your home.

- Prevention is better – and cheaper – than a cure. Prevent pipes from freezing in winter, for example, by putting the plugs into baths and basins, which will keep out cold air; by throwing a handful of salt down the drains last thing at night; and by insulating pipes with foam held in place with adhesive tape. Note, too, that the heat generated by leaving one light bulb on at night during very cold weather is often enough to stop pipes freezing.

A handful of salt down the plughole on a frosty night will prevent pipes freezing.

- An airlock can occur in a water pipe if a large amount of water is suddenly drawn off the system. To remove the air, cover a mallet in a towel and then gently tap along the length of the pipe with it.

- Never touch electrical equipment, sockets or switches with wet hands, feet or clothes, and always wear shoes when switching on electrical appliances.

- Have electrical appliances regularly serviced and repaired (especially if there are any frayed or worn cables) by a qualified electrician.

- Unplug all appliances when they are not in use and switch off the television at the wall socket and unplug it at night. Not only is this a safety precaution, but it will also save energy (even the little red light on appliances that indicates that the power is on is using electricity and thus costing you money).

Switch off and unplug electrical appliances from sockets when not in use and at night.

- Do not overload adaptors in case you overload the electrical system.
- If you smell a fishy or burning odour, an appliance's plug may be overheating and starting to melt. Switch off the appliance immediately and remove the plug from the socket.
- If a plug feels warm, switch off the appliance and remove the plug from the wall socket. Then turn off the power at the consumer unit (the fuse box) and call an electrician.
- It's vital to use the correct fire extinguisher to dampen down electrical fires, so if you don't have one, buy one!
- Fit a smoke alarm and make sure that you regularly check and change its batteries. Doing so will safeguard the lives of those in your house, and for a very small amount of money.
- If a power cut does strike, turn off all appliances and light switches (apart from one light switch and the fridge and freezer) because if a power surge occurs when the electricity supply is restored, it may cause fuses to blow. After the power has been restored, reset any electrical timer switches and clocks and keep the freezer closed for at least six hours to compensate for its earlier loss of cooling power.
- If you smell gas, extinguish any cigarettes, candles, gas stoves and pilot lights on cookers and boilers. Switch off any machinery that may generate sparks and don't switch any lights on or off. Do not enter a suspect building or room to investigate the cause of a gas leak in case you are overcome by toxic fumes. Turn off the gas supply by closing the valve next to your gas meter, open as many windows as possible, evacuate the building and warn your neighbours. Then call the gas company and stay outside until it advises you that it's safe to re-enter your house.

Make sure that candles and matches are accessible in case of a power cut.

DIY top tips

These top tips will make doing it yourself both easier and more effective.

> If you can't hold a small nail or tack between your finger and thumb when hammering it, push it through a piece of cardboard – holding the cardboard when hammering will ensure that you won't hit your thumb.

- Rather than hammering nails in a straight line along the grain of a piece of wood, stagger the nails to prevent the wood from splitting.
- Always hammer a nail through a thinner piece of wood into a thicker one, if possible using a nail that is three times as long as the thinner piece of wood.
- If you dip the tips of screws and nails in petroleum jelly or press them into a bar of soap before use, it will lessen the resistance when they are used and the wood is less likely to split. Once greased, the nails are preserved against rust and will be easier to remove.

Hammer nails through the thinner piece of wood into the thicker pieces.

> Dipping the tips of screws and nails in petroleum jelly or pressing them into a bar of soap will lessen the resistance when hammering them into wood and thus discourage the wood from splitting. It will also prevent them from rusting and will make them easier to remove if you need to.

- Loosen rusted screws or nails by putting a drop of vinegar on their heads and leaving it to soak in. For rusted bolts, try a thick coating of cola.
- To tighten a loose screw, remove it and glue a wooden matchstick into the hole before replacing the screw.
- Not sure in which direction to turn a screw? If so, remember this: 'Left is loose, right is tight'!
- Turn off stopcocks and water taps by twisting them in a clockwise direction.
- A length of pencil stub cut to size makes a good alternative to a Rawlplug (a hook or screw will easily penetrate its soft graphite).
- Plasterboard stud partition walls won't support any weight, so if you want to hang a shelf from one you will have to locate its wooden studs and drive your screws and nails into those. Locate the studs by using a directional compass: pass the compass slowly across the wall, and when the needle moves you'll know that you've found a stud (the compass reacts to the metal nails driven into it).

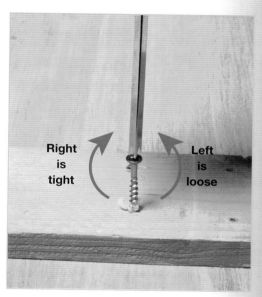

Right is tight / Left is loose

- You will need to find a joist (which will run at right angles to the floorboards of the room above) if you want to fix anything into a ceiling. Find out the rough location of a joist by tapping the ceiling: an echoing sound indicates a cavity, while a dull sound signals a joist. Then use a bradawl or small drill to confirm the location of the joist.

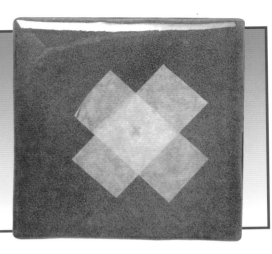

Applying a masking-tape cross to the surface of a tile, wall or piece of wood is the best way of preventing an electric-drill bit from slipping off the mark.

- If you need to drive a nail into a plaster wall – to hang a picture, for example – first apply two lengths of sticky tape to the wall in the form of a cross to mark where the nail should go. Doing this will prevent the plaster from cracking.
- Add plaster – or any other dry ingredient – to water, not water to plaster, to avoid the mixture ending up too lumpy or wet.
- Run out of filler? If so, fill small holes made by nails and screws and fine cracks with white toothpaste, which will dry to a rock-hard consistency.
- Remove splashes of paint or cement from bricks by rubbing them with another brick.
- Note that saw blades will glide better if you rub both sides with an old candle.

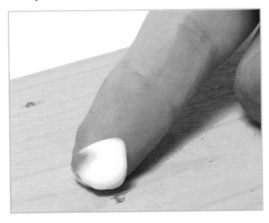

White toothpaste can be used as an emergency wood filler for small holes.

- Remember that successful sawing involves applying pressure on the downward stroke.

- Don't paint straight over knots in wood, especially the untreated wood that is used for flat-pack furniture, because the resinous sap will continue to seep out, staining the paint. Instead, give knots a coat of knotting solution first.

- Light bulbs will last longer if you dust them (a build-up of dust tends to cause them to overheat and then blow).

Saw blades glide more easily if rubbed with a wax candle first.

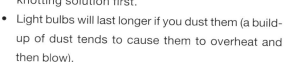

- If a light bulb breaks while you are removing it from its fitting, leaving a jagged edge of glass, pressing a large, dry bar of soap firmly over the 'stump' will give you enough leverage to remove the remains of the bulb from the fitting. (Discard the soap afterwards.)

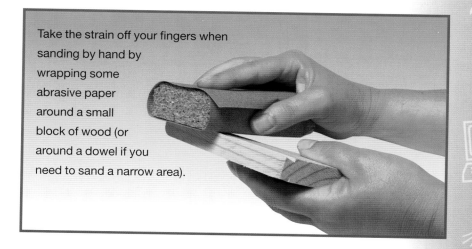

Take the strain off your fingers when sanding by hand by wrapping some abrasive paper around a small block of wood (or around a dowel if you need to sand a narrow area).

- Sprinkling talcum powder into the joints and gaps between floorboards can stop any squeaks and creaks.
- Silence creaking hinges by rubbing them with a little petroleum jelly, a pencil (as you would a sticking zip) or washing-up liquid.
- Cure a sticking door by rubbing chalk down the edge that meets the frame and then closing it. When you reopen the door, the part of the frame that is causing the problem will be marked with chalk, identifying the section that you should rub down with abrasive paper.
- Rubbing their runners with a candle or a little moist stop will make sliding doors and drawers glide more easily.

CONSERVING ENERGY

Energy wastage means money wastage, so follow these tips and safeguard your purse.

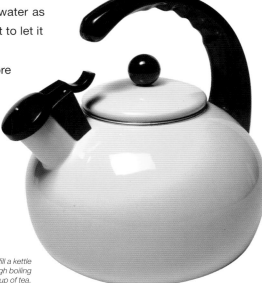

- Fill kettles with only as much water as you need – why heat water just to let it go cold again?
- Remember that freezers are more economical to run if they are full – even if they're only full of ice cubes.
- Check that you are not overheating your rooms: a rise of 1°C (2°F) on the thermostat setting will send up heating costs by 10 per cent.

Save energy and money: don't fill a kettle to the top if you just need enough boiling water for one cup of tea.

- Note that thermostats react to hot and cold spots, so that a sudden rush of cold air in a hallway, or even the heat generated by a hi-fi, television or table lamp, will affect a thermostat in the vicinity.
- Placing radiator foil behind radiators can save up to 15 per cent of heating costs.
- Note that curtains, furniture and carpets restrict heat flow, while drawing curtains over radiators will direct heat onto windowpanes, not into rooms.
- To prevent heat loss, ensure that your hot-water cylinder is adequately lagged.
- The areas of insulation that are most often overlooked are the hot-water pipes that lead from hot-water cylinders to taps. If you lag these, not only will the water stay hotter for longer, but you'll save money, too.
- Showers are more economical and waste less energy than baths (four people can shower in the same amount of water that one person needs for a bath). Alternatively, if you prefer baths, take one with a friend!
- It's worth checking that the hot-water pipes beneath floorboards are adequately lagged and to remedy the situation if they are not.
- If you plan to lay insulating blanket in the loft, don't open the specially packaged bags that contain it until you get them up there because as soon as they are opened the contents will expand enormously.
- Because insulation materials can cause skin irritation, wear both gloves and a dust mask when handling them.

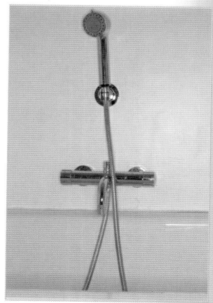

Showers are more economical than baths: you'll use less water and save money on heating the water you do use.

- When in the loft, make sure that you have adequate light to work by and don't step, stand or walk in the area between the joists because the rafters will rarely be able support your weight and you may end up falling through the ceiling into the room below. Instead, spread your weight evenly by placing a couple of planks across the joists and also wear kneepads when working.

- To prevent them from freezing, don't forget to lag the cold-water tank and the pipes leading from it. In fact, you must do this by law in the UK, and buying a Bylaw 30 insulation kit will ensure that you have everything you need with which to insulate your tank. Remember never to place any insulation material directly beneath the tank because if it isn't obstructed, the small amount of warm air that rises up through the house will keep the tank frost-free.

- Plan ahead: the best bargains in insulation are offered by DIY stores in summer.

- Although double-glazing can reduce heat loss significantly, the payback time – the time needed to recoup the cost of installation – is long. Improvise instead by blocking draughts by fitting self-adhesive foam strips along any gaps and by keeping in heat by hanging snuggly fitting, closely woven curtains and drawing them at night. It's also worth considering fitting renewable 'clingfilm' double-glazing (available from DIY stores), which is easy to fit and requires only the heat of a hairdryer to shrink it to a tight fit.

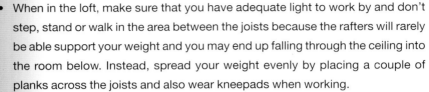

Remember that cork tiles are warmer on the feet than vinyl. They are also simple to lay and can be sealed to make them easier to clean (but don't seal cork tiles in bathrooms because their absorbent qualities are helpful in steamy atmospheres).

GREEN FINGERS

No matter where you live, there is always room for some plants or flowers. Plants offer the perfect way of introducing colour and scent to your home: the simplest window box transforms a dull view; a hanging basket adds a welcome splash of summer colour to a back door; while a kitchen windowsill lined with pots of tasty culinary herbs or bright blooms makes cooking – and washing up afterwards – more of a pleasure than a chore.

CARING FOR FLOWERS

Few things in life can beat the uplifting feeling of receiving a bunch of flowers, but it seems that the best way of treating a bouquet is to insult the person who gave them to you. In The Netherlands, people never thank someone for a floral gift as if it were just a present, but instead lavish adoring words on the greenery – not the donor – so that the plants will 'feel special'! Similarly, if you receive a bunch of flowers as a gift, don't immediately arrange the flowers in a vase, but instead dump them in a bucket full of cold water and then put them in a cupboard or the bathroom. Be sure to explain to the person who gave them to you that the flowers are doubtless thirsty after their journey, which is why you're giving them a long, overnight drink in a cool, dark place.

Place bunches of flowers immediately into a bucket of cold water to let them recover.

Here are some more tips to help you to make the most of your flowers.

- Pick flowers from your garden in the early morning or evening because flowers that are picked when the sun is full will wither more rapidly, as will those that are picked when it's raining heavily.

A beautiful flower arrangement can last longer with a little care and attention.

- Don't buy flowers on Mondays because they are likely to have been left over from Saturday's delivery. Choose flowers that are still in bud (these will be the youngest in the florist's) and check that the stems look fresh below the water line. Don't buy flowers that have dark, slimy stems, dull petals or pollen that falls off easily because these are signs that they have spent a long time in the shop.
- If you love flowers, don't give them a sauna! Cellophane-wrapped flowers may look glamorous, but the cellophane dehydrates them to the extent of halving their lifespan, so ask the florist to wrap them in paper instead.
- The first step to take with bought flowers is to recut all of their stems (which may have become dry) to enable them to suck up water. (In Japan, flower stems are cut under water so that no bubbles of air can be trapped in the stem and thus obstruct the flow of water to the flower head.)

Cutting the stems of flowers under water stops air bubbles getting trapped in the stems.

- If flower stems start bleeding white sap after you've cut them, sear them with a flame.
- Woody stemmed flowers (apart from roses) will benefit from having the end of their stems bashed a bit.
- Strip off any leaves that would otherwise be beneath the water line in a vase. If you leave them on, they'll rot and the flowers won't last as long.
- Note that short-stemmed flowers will last longer if they are placed in a bowl of wet sand rather than a vase or bowl of water.
- If a simple bunch of flowers looks a little forlorn, make the arrangement more exciting by adding some greenery – parsley, rosemary and lavender work wonders!
- Once you've installed the flowers in a vase, change the water every day. Trimming off a small piece of each stem daily will also keep flowers fresh for as long as possible.
- If you can't change the water every day, place a piece of charcoal or a copper coin in the flower water.
- Exchanging their water for lemonade seems to revive roses, chrysanthemums and carnations that appear on the verge of giving up the ghost. If you don't have any lemonade, try adding a crushed aspirin to fresh water, but don't give flowers a pill unless it seems necessary because it may harm healthy blooms.

- Wilted flowers can sometimes be successfully revived by placing them in a plastic bag with a couple of apple slices.
- Preserve that extra-special single bloom indefinitely by placing it in a jar or bottle filled with surgical spirit and then sealing the container.

Strip off leaves that would be below the water line in vases to keep the flowers lasting longer.

CARNATIONS

Carnations are loners that hate sharing vases with other blooms. Buy them when their buds are tightly closed, break, rather than cut, their stems between two nodes (the knobbly protrusions on their stems) and then let them sit in a bucket of cold water for an hour before arranging them.

Floral TLC

Although tulips and daffodils may seem made for each other, the truth is that they hate being in close proximity and shouldn't therefore share the same vase. Here are some further tips on which flowers to separate and which to combine, as well as how to care for them.

Chrysanthemums

- To prepare chrysanthemums, hammer the bottom of their stems and dip them in very hot water for a couple of minutes before standing them up to their necks in cool water. Because the leaves rot very easily, make sure that you strip the stems bare and then rub them smooth. Chrysanthemums should have their water changed daily.

Foxgloves

- Friendly foxgloves will prolong the lives of their companions in the same vase of water.

Gerberas

- Gerberas (which come from South Africa and look like giant daisies) need special treatment. Because their stems rot very quickly when under water, don't give them a long drink and instead place them in a jug or bucket filled with 1 cm (1/2 in) of boiling water for a couple of hours to stiffen the stems. When arranged in a vase, the water should not reach higher than a quarter of their stem length to keep any rotting to a minimum.

Gladioli

- Gladioli are among the most easy-going of flowers, despite being a little on the tall side for most people's vases. Cut their stems under water and then recut them every three or four days. If you nip out the top bud and remove the lower blooms as they wilt, you'll help your 'gladies' to keep blooming.

Irises and lilies

- Irises and lilies should be bought when in bud. Both like having their stems cut at an angle, while removing any wilting blooms will encourage new ones to open. Both tend to foul their water quickly, so change it daily. Be warned that lilies' pollen will stain fabrics, so keep them well away from soft furnishings.

Lupins

- Lupins (like tulips) continue to grow in the vase, which is why they twist and turn out of position after you've arranged them. If treated well, lupins can last for weeks. Cut the tips of their stems and then let them stand overnight in a bucket of water (which should reach to their lowest blooms). The next day, dissolve a large tablespoonful of sugar in 500 ml (1 pint) of warm water, cut each stem to the required length, pour some of the sugar solution up each cut stem and finally firmly plug the ends with cotton wool. This rather fiddly treatment will benefit all hollow-stemmed flowers, including delphiniums.

Nasturtiums

- Note that nasty nasturtiums will destroy other types of flower in the same vase.

Spring flowers

- Flowers produced by spring bulbs, such as daffodils, narcissi and tulips, are among the few that do mind sharing the same water. Cut the stems well above the white part and then rinse them thoroughly under a cold tap. If they look like they're flagging, add a generous pinch of salt to their water to revive them, but don't change the water (which they prefer shallow) and don't recut their stems.

Stocks

- Sweetly scented stocks can be serial killers: because their leaves and stems rot quickly under water, they will swiftly poison any other flowers that share the same vase. To prepare them, cut and hammer their stems, dip the tips in boiling water for a minute, remove every bit of leaf from the stems and then give them a long, cool drink and leave them overnight. The next day, add a copper coin and 5 ml (a teaspoon) of sugar to the water in the vase and then remember to change it daily.

Roses

- Roses are picky, so please them by cutting their stems at an angle under water and then slitting the bottom 2.5 cm (1 in). Don't hammer them – they hate it! Next, having protected the blooms from the steam, place a paperbag over the blooms and plunge the stem tips into boiling water for a minute or two and then stand the roses in a bucket filled with cool water overnight. Before transferring

them to a vase (they dislike florist's oasis), remove any leaves that would otherwise be submerged below the water line and then remember to top up their water daily. If a rose's head starts to droop, the stem may contain an airlock (which often happens when stems have been hammered). Revive the rose either by recutting the stem tip and plunging it into boiling water; by poking a pin through the rose's bent neck; or by recutting the stem, rolling it up in newspaper with its head pointing upwards and then leaving it to sit in warm water (which should reach up to its neck) overnight.

Sweetly scented and beautifully coloured, roses do need a little extra care to keep them happy.

Tulips

- Tulips are troublesome because they carry on growing in the vase and thus changing shape. Open tulips (but not those in bud) can be made to conform, however, by cutting their stems straight across, rolling the bunch tightly in newspaper and then standing the package in a bucket of warm water overnight. When placing them in a vase, gently stroke the stems into your preferred position; you could also gently stroke the petals to encourage the upward curve from the base to become reversed so that the blooms display their brilliantly exotic inner markings. However you arrange them, tulips seem to last longer if you prick their stems just below the water line, add a little sugar or a copper coin to their water and then don't change it.

Violets

- Violets (but not African violets) drink water through their floral faces, which means that they'll last longer if you place them face down in water overnight before arranging them in wet sand. Spraying them daily with cool water will also encourage them to last longer.

CARING FOR HOUSEPLANTS

Keep your houseplants healthy and looking their best with the following tips.

Because a layer of dust on plant leaves can filter out as much as 50 per cent of the light that indoor plants need, regularly give them a light dusting.

- It's best to water house plants with rainwater, but if you do use tap water, let it stand for a couple of days at room temperature, both to warm it up (indoor plants loathe the shock of cold water) and to let any chemicals settle.
- Starch is a great nutrient for plants, so for a special plant treat, the next time you boil some potatoes or pasta, reserve, cool and then save the water to give to them.
- Like people, plants need company, so arrange them in groups.
- Help to maintain a mini-greenhouse atmosphere by lightly misting groups of plants with a plant-sprayer.

- Once a plant is happy in a particular place, don't move it, apart from turning it around regularly to encourage even growth and prevent it from leaning towards the light.

A light spray will help maintain a mini-greenhouse atmosphere.

- Don't leave houseplants on windowsills on winter nights unless you have blinds or don't draw your curtains because drawn curtains will trap cold air around the plants and thus kill them.

Maintain the shine on a house plant's leaves by gently wiping them with a soft cloth to which a few drops of glycerine have been added. Alternatively, try wiping either the inside of a banana skin or a little beer over them.

If a house plant's surface soil becomes dry and crusted, water will simply run off it, eventually causing the plant to die of thirst. Remedy the situation by gently loosening the soil as much as possible – an old table fork is the best tool for this task – and then giving the plant a thorough watering.

- African violets are delightful house plants, but many people kill them because they don't realise that they hate getting their leaves wet. Water an African violet by standing its pot in water overnight to enable it to soak up as much moisture as it needs and then allow the pot to drain the next morning. African violets seem to like a little extra calcium, so after boiling eggs, save, cool and reserve the water for them. These plants will adore a sunny spot, but in the absence of sunshine, try positioning them under a table lamp.

- Falling ferns can be nursed back to health by watering them with some diluted black tea or coffee once a month.

- Before going away on holiday, make sure that your plants will be well looked

after. If you can't find someone to come in and water them for you, place several layers of newspaper – or even better, an old towel – in the bathtub and fill the bath with cold water to a level of 5 cm (2 inches). Then position the plants on the newspaper or towel, having first made sure that the drainage holes in their pots are large enough to enable them to take up the water.

- If you have a really big indoor plant that's too large to move to the bathtub, water it in your absence by first twisting a length of cloth and then burying one end to a depth of several inches in the plant's soil and dropping the other end in a large container of water set slightly higher than the plant pot. The water from the container will then be transferred along the cloth and into the soil by osmosis.

- Overwatering is as lethal to house plants as underwatering, while depending on the humidity in its part of the room, one plant may need a different watering regime to another of the same species across the room.

- Azaleas enjoy spending the summer outdoors, so move them outside when you switch off your central heating and bring them in when you turn it on again in autumn. Note that letting the roots of indoor azaleas dry out is the most common cause of their demise.

Sink your finger into a pot plant's soil to see whether it needs watering. If it feels dry, water it; if not, test it again in a few days.

Potting-on and other maintenance tips

If roots start to grow through the drainage holes in the base of the pot, it's a sure sign that a house plant is becoming pot-bound and needs repotting. A plant in a pot relies on you for nourishment, and when it has outgrown its pot, it will need a new and bigger one, as well as fresh food in the form of potting compost. Repot a

pot-bound house plant into a pot that is one size larger than the previous one, preferably in the spring. The longer you keep a pot in a container, the higher the number of the John Innes compost that you will need, with No 3 being required for long-term pot residents. Don't reuse old compost because the nutrients will have been used up and there may also be organisms of disease lurking within it.

Time to move on: When roots emerge through drainage holes, the plant needs a bigger pot.

Here are some more tips with which to cherish pot plants.

- Shops often sell arrangements consisting of several different species of plant in the same container. Although they make an attractive combination, some of the plants may require different conditions and watering regimes to others. Once the initial appeal has worn off, it's therefore best to transfer the plants to individual pots.

- Before carrying it home, always protect a newly purchased house plant by wrapping it up, especially in cold weather.

- If you have an enormous specimen that is taking over your home, don't chop it back because this will probably kill it. Instead, advertise it: such house plants are not only valuable, but much sought-after for offices, atria and other large spaces.

Re-pot plants into the next size pot and use a good quality compost to provide nutrients.

CONTAINER GARDENS

- Container gardens make excellent alternatives – or additions – to the real thing, but require special treatment.
- Note that a pot or container that holds less compost than a conventional 20 cm (8 in) diameter pot will need frequent watering in summer.
- If the compost's surface level is about 2 or 3 cm (1 in) below the rim of a container or pot, it will enable you to water it without washing away the compost.
- Every month or so, prick over the compost of any containers or tubs in which long-standing residents are growing to prevent it from becoming compacted, thereby stopping it from absorbing air, water and nutrients.

All sorts of buckets, barrels, pots and containers can make an attractive feature in even the smallest garden.

- If you live in a flat, or have access to a flat roof, check any weight restrictions before installing large containers in it. It's worth remembering that 1 cubic metre of compost weighs 1 tonne – and that's only its dry weight! If you then add the weight of a container, plants and water, you could be placing an intolerable strain on the floor, which may not be able to support it.
- Before installing a window box, check that you are allowed to have one. Certain local authorities in the UK have banned them, while some landlords fear that they will damage the structure of their buildings. In fact, a well-prepared window box will not cause any damage as long as it is anchored firmly in place (you can buy special brackets to do this) and has a drip tray to catch any excess water that drains out of it. And not only are they attractive, but window boxes make it difficult for intruders to climb in through windows – they'd have to tackle the plants first!

- When planting up a window box, remember that you are creating a miniature landscape. Consider including some dwarf or slow-growing plants, such as conifers, and one or two trailing ivies to soften the edges. Add splashes of colour by introducing some summer bedding plants – perhaps petunias – winter-flowering pansies or miniature cyclamen or a few dwarf tulip bulbs, which will give you a welcome surprise in spring.

- Don't forget that the plants in window boxes need food and water and that they will need to be dug up, potted on and replaced by smaller specimens when they grow too big. So make sure that you feed and water window boxes regularly and that you change the compost – and plants – when necessary.

- Note that although they are heavier than their plastic counterparts, clay pots are better at maintaining the correct soil–air relationship. They need regular watering in dry weather, but are less likely to become waterlogged and thus damage a plant's roots than plastic pots.

- Before buying them, make sure that terracotta pots, troughs and ornaments are frost-proof, otherwise they won't be suitable for outside use in winter.

Note that stacking up terracotta pots, especially large ones, can cause them to crack. Avert the danger of them becoming jammed together by placing a few sheets of newspaper between each pair of pots.

- Wooden half-barrels are among the cheapest forms of really large container, but need to be lined with plastic sheets (with some drainage holes punched into the plastic sheets and the barrel) to prevent them from rotting. Unless you are planting a tree, you won't need to fill the entire barrel with compost. Instead, fill the bottom half with a layer of broken shards of pot to provide drainage, then add some ordinary garden soil before topping up the barrel with compost to an adequate rooting depth.

- Remember that a large pot filled with compost and plants will be very heavy, so save yourself the struggle of moving it by selecting your preferred location and positioning the pot there before filling it.

- Some containers may be so heavy that they are nearly impossible to move. Indeed, lengths of scaffolding poles may be the only things strong enough to bear their weight (and will also act as rollers). It's vital that you don't attempt to move such large containers on your own, however, and that you instead get help.

- To obtain an aged appearance, simply paint garden ornaments and pots with a little milk. This will encourage moss to grow on them, and they'll soon look as though they've been there for years.

An old tin tub rescued from the rubbish tip is given a new lease of life as the home for your summer bedding plants.

- For maximum impact, group pots and containers of varying sizes together (single pots can look a little lonely, and plants like to have company).
- You'll find hanging baskets hard to lift unless you plant them up and position them before watering them. Lightweight, soil-less compost, which has been specially designed for hanging baskets, is also well worth investing in.
- Watering hanging baskets can be tricky, not least because they need plenty of water (even when it's raining). Mixing water-retaining gel with the compost when planting up the hanging basket will help it to retain moisture for longer.
- Inserting a kitchen funnel into the compost and then placing the nozzle of a watering can into that makes directing water into hanging baskets easier. An even easier method is to place ice cubes on the surface of the compost and then to leave them to melt (indeed, this is the only way of ensuring that water doesn't dribble down your arm!)
- If you are going away for a few days, keep a hanging basket well watered by filling a clean, empty bottle of washing-up liquid with water, inverting it and then inserting it into the compost, hiding the bottle among the flowers and foliage. The tiny drip, drip, drip of water from the nozzle will slowly penetrate the compost.

Even the smallest space can make a garden. Here an old bench is pressed into service to display cut blooms.

IN THE GARDEN

If you are are uncertain about what to grow – or what will grow in your type of soil – ask your neighbours. Gardening is as much about friendship as it is about plants, and you'll probably soon find yourself sharing and trading plants. When visiting other people's gardens, make a note of the plants that you like and then talk to the experts in your local garden centre or nursery to glean advice about them.

Gardening on any scale is fun. It's also a great way to get neighbours talking to each other!

Here are some more tried-and-tested garden tips and advice.

- Note that although it is illegal to dig up wild plants and flowers, most wild species are available as seeds for garden cultivation (albeit often from specialist nurseries), while a friendly neighbour may have a spare such plant that has made its home in his or her garden.

- Don't bring any plants or plant material home with you from a holiday abroad, not least because there are strict regulations governing the importation of plants to avoid spreading disease and to protect indigenous species from foreign invaders. If you do wish to purchase plants abroad, however, obtain them from a reputable nursery that will guarantee that they are disease-free, will provide the correct documentation for the plants' exportation to your home country and will also arrange for them to be shipped.

- Never collect rocks, stones or pebbles from the countryside or a beach to put in your garden. Not only is this illegal, but it is also environmental vandalism! Most garden centres stock a wonderful range of rocks, stones and pebbles, which they'll probably deliver to your home, too.

- Before buying a tree or shrub, always read its label or tag to ascertain how high it will grow and how wide it will spread. Remember that a small shrub may grow into a huge plant within a couple of years, and if this is likely, ensure that you plant it in an appropriate place, and somewhere it will not affect your neighbour's house or view. The same goes for climbers: although you may yearn for roses around your door, your immediate neighbour may not (particularly if you

Water is a plant nutrient and valuable commodity, so don't waste it.

live in a semi-detached house, but try telling that to a plant!)

- At the height of summer, it's worth making a written record of those plants that need moving or dividing because once autumn comes, you'll find it impossible to remember which ones need attention.

- If a particular species of plant has died, don't plant another of the same species in the same spot. The chances are that the plant died because it wasn't happy where it was, but it could also have contracted a disease that will continue to affect the soil – and the species of plant that is grown in it – for some time to come.

- Water is both a plant nutrient and a valuable commodity that must not be wasted. Before watering the garden with a hose pipe, make sure that you are acting within the law because hose-pipe bans are common in many places during the summer months and some local authorities in the UK require you to purchase a hose-pipe licence. In most places, you must furthermore have a non-return valve fitted to any tap to which a hose is attached to prevent drinking water from becoming contaminated. If possible, collect rainwater in a covered butt for use in the garden.

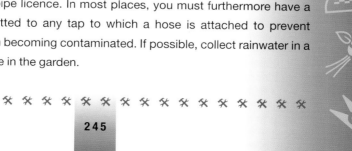

- Always water your garden in the evening in hot weather so that it has a chance to soak into your plants' roots before evaporating in the heat of the day.
- Hydrangeas will drink almost anything happily, even a bowl of cold water in which the dishes have been washed. If you want a pink hydrangea, sprinkle the plant with lime; for a blue one, add a little aluminium sulphate to the water.
- If you are right-handed, the right-hand glove of a pair of gardening gloves tends to wear out first, but rather than throwing away the perfectly serviceable left-hand one, too, turn it inside out to act as a new right-hand glove.

Don't use power garden tools on Sundays, especially Sunday afternoons. Sundays are traditionally a time to sit and enjoy the peace and tranquillity of your garden, not a time to annoy your neighbours.

Top garden tips

Did you know that hollyhocks love beer, or that camellias are teetotal (but that tea leaves make a perfect mulch for them)? Here are some more fascinating tips, as well as some safety hints.

- Digging baked banana skins into the soil around rose beds provides potassium.
- Do you desire brighter-yellow daffodils? If so, mix some dry mustard powder with your fertiliser when planting the bulbs.
- Flies and mosquitoes hate mint, so rub a couple of leaves over your exposed limbs before working in the garden.
- Placing crushed mothballs on flowerbeds will force dogs to do a U-turn at the first sniff.
- Crumbling and scattering some dried orange or lemon peel around bedding plants will keep cats away from them.
- Look to your safety when pruning trees and anchor your ladder securely.
- Wear goggles when pruning or cutting hedges.
- Only apply chemicals to your garden that have been specifically sold for garden use, follow the instructions on their labels carefully, never store them in anything other than their original packaging and keep them out of children and pets' reach.
- Always label containers that have been used for spreading weedkillers and never use them for watering or applying other chemical treatments.
- If you have pets, use liquid chemical solutions to prevent their paws from picking up powdered fertilisers and weedkillers.
- Never spray garden chemicals when the weather is windy or frosty.
- Wear gloves when gardening, partly because the sap of some plants – including poinsettias and oleanders – can cause skin irritation, and partly because you'll save your hands from being impaled by splinters and prevent cuts from becoming ingrained with, and infected, by soil.

Be careful when handling cacti (even those that don't seem to have many obvious spines because they may be hidden under the woolly mass on the surface). The animal equivalent of cacti are the very hairy 'woolly-bear' caterpillars, whose hairs can cause nasty skin irritations when they come into contact with human skin.

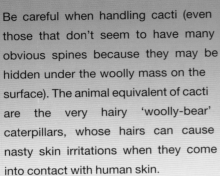

- Remember that many plants are toxic. Laburnum seeds, yews and foxgloves, for example, can all be dangerously poisonous and are therefore best removed from gardens if you have small children who may ingest them.
- Don't eat mushrooms or toadstools that you've found on your lawn, or anywhere else, before having had them properly identified by an acknowledged authority.

Don't collect or eat fungi that you find - they may be toxic.

EASY-GOING, EASY-GROWING HERBS

Herbs are some of the easiest plants to grow, as well as some of the most forgiving – they actually prefer to live in poor soil and not to be watered a lot. They are furthermore probably the most useful to have around, be it for use in the kitchen, in the wardrobe or in the bath.

Although it is possible to grow many herbs from seed, some need encouraging in order to germinate (parsley seeds, for instance, need to be covered in boiling water to get them going). Annual herbs – those that last for only one

Culinary herbs are easy to grow in pots on a bright kitchen windowsill.

season – are generally the easiest to grow from seed, and these include dill, coriander, chervil, salad rocket, borage (the flowers look lovely when frozen in ice cubes and dropped into long drinks), sweet marjoram and mustard. You can also grow a few perennial herbs from seed without too much trouble, such as chives, oregano, French marjoram and sage.

Almost all herbs, however, are better bought as plants that have been grown from cuttings. You won't have to wait for them to germinate before enjoying them and, given the space, a perennial herb will carry on for years. As you get to know your herbs, you can start to make your own cuttings, be it to increase your stock, to give as gifts or to replace older specimens that have done their duty and served you well, but that have now passed their best.

Here are some useful hints to help you to make the most of your herbs.

- Some herbs self-seed, that is, they cast their seeds about quite freely, allowing the plants to spread. Fennel is possibly the most prolific self-seeder, but if you want to admire the attractive-looking bronze version only, you'll have to weed out its green offspring.

✻ ✻

- Garlic grows well in a pot on the windowsill. When harvesting your crop, leave a length – 25 to 28 cm (8 to 10 in) – of dried stem attached to each bulb to plait together so that you can store your garlic both attractively and practically.

- Mint is a vigorous plant, and if you plant it directly into the soil, you'll end up with a garden in which mint is running rampant. To avert this scenario, only grow mint in pots (terracotta ones are the best because these forceful plants can burst through plastic ones) sunk into holes in the garden and lift the pots every autumn to trim off any shoots that are threatening to make a run for it and escape. An eau de cologne made of mint is wonderfully refreshing in the bath; to make the best mint sauce for lamb, use the woolly leaved apple mint; and try garnishing new potatoes with spearmint.

- Thyme comes in many varieties, some spreading, some bushy. The best in terms of both flavour and appearance is the bushy 'Silver posy'.

- Rosemary is one of the happiest of herbs: all that it asks for is soil and a bit of sunshine, although, like lavender, it hates having wet roots and prefers a well-drained soil. Both rosemary and lavender flower, and as soon as the flowers have faded, give the plants a haircut by cutting back the stems – but avoid cutting into the woody parts – to keep their form round and bushy. (If you don't trim them, they'll grow tall and leggy.

- Basil is beautiful, but sadly one of the few herbs that is not hardy in British climates. You can, however, grow basil from seed each year as an annual and then pot up a few plants for indoor use (keep some in the kitchen with which to banish flies). If you pinch out the growing tips, you'll have lovely, bushy plants that will keep you well supplied with the primary ingredient of pesto sauce throughout the winter.

- If you don't have the space to grow herbs in winter, the simplest way of preserving them is to freeze them.

INDEX

accessories 161–162
ammonia 18, 39
amyl acetate 139
apples 92
aubergine 103

baking soda - see bicarbonate of soda
bananas 93–94
bathroom 65–69
bedding 16, 35, 64
bedrooms 63–64
beeswax polish 24, 54
bicarbonate of soda 17, 38, 36, 58, 67, 69, 73, 75, 106, 118, 145
bleach 42, 68
blinds 47
body treatments 174–176
books 59
borax 18
brass 15, 59
bread 110
broccoli 107
brushes 12, 13
buckets 13

candles 35, 37
carpets 30-32
carpet stains 34–39
carrots 94
ceilings 40
celery 95
ceramic tiles 42
chalk 84
chopping boards 84
chrome 60
cigarette smoke 61, 62
cleaning equipment 12, 13, 14,15 (see also individual entries)
cleaning products 16–18
clothes 10, 127–162
    care labels 128–131
    storage 155–158
clutter 9, 10
coffee grounds 62
cola 83, 221
cookers 71–74
copper 15
crayons 25
crockery 78, 79
curtains 45–48
    lace 47
    net 47
    voiles 47
    washing 46
cutlery 79, 117

damp 59
deodoriser 14
dishwashers 74, 80
DIY 189–226
    safety 191
    tips 217–224
drains 71
dry-cleaning 132, 139
    fluid 25
dusting 25, 40
dustpan 13

e numbers 89–91
eggs 100, 103, 115–117, 126
electrical appliances 71, 75–77 (see also individual entries)
electricity 218, 219
energy conservation 224–225

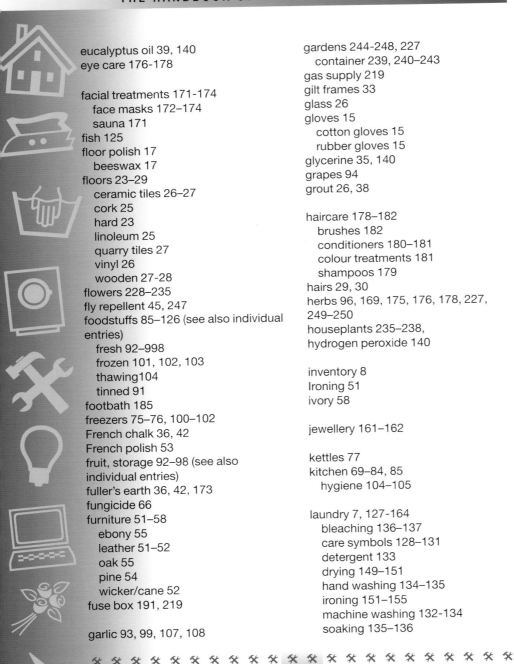

eucalyptus oil 39, 140
eye care 176-178

facial treatments 171-174
   face masks 172–174
   sauna 171
fish 125
floor polish 17
   beeswax 17
floors 23–29
   ceramic tiles 26–27
   cork 25
   hard 23
   linoleum 25
   quarry tiles 27
   vinyl 26
   wooden 27-28
flowers 228–235
fly repellent 45, 247
foodstuffs 85–126 (see also individual entries)
   fresh 92–998
   frozen 101, 102, 103
   thawing104
   tinned 91
footbath 185
freezers 75–76, 100–102
French chalk 36, 42
French polish 53
fruit, storage 92–98 (see also individual entries)
fuller's earth 36, 42, 173
fungicide 66
furniture 51–58
   ebony 55
   leather 51–52
   oak 55
   pine 54
   wicker/cane 52
fuse box 191, 219

garlic 93, 99, 107, 108

gardens 244-248, 227
   container 239, 240–243
gas supply 219
gilt frames 33
glass 26
gloves 15
   cotton gloves 15
   rubber gloves 15
glycerine 35, 140
grapes 94
grout 26, 38

haircare 178–182
   brushes 182
   conditioners 180–181
   colour treatments 181
   shampoos 179
hairs 29, 30
herbs 96, 169, 175, 176, 178, 227, 249–250
houseplants 235–238,
hydrogen peroxide 140

inventory 8
Ironing 51
ivory 58

jewellery 161–162

kettles 77
kitchen 69–84, 85
   hygiene 104–105

laundry 7, 127-164
   bleaching 136–137
   care symbols 128–131
   detergent 133
   drying 149–151
   hand washing 134–135
   ironing 151–155
   machine washing 132-134
   soaking 135–136

lavatories 68
lavender bags 62
lemon 16, 59, 65, 72, 82, 84, 94, 95, 99, 137
lettuce 94, 125
lime-scale 15, 65 66
    remover 60, 66, 69

marble 58
mattress 16, 65
meat 102, 105, 120–123
    roasting times 122–123
melons 93, 99
methylated spirits 37
microwave ovens 74
milk 36, 106, 118, 126
mirrors 17, 26, 43–44
mop 16
mops 11, 12
    dry mop 12
    sponge mops 11
moths 62
mould 66
mouthwash 67
mushrooms 97, 108

nailbrush 11
nails 186
nail polish 29, 147

odours 61-62, 69, 62 69, 84, 99, 108
    foot 185
oil paintings 33
oils, essential 176, 176, 179
olives 97
olive oil 97, 114
onions 97. 108
organisation 6–11
ovens - see cooker

paint 192–195,
    applicators 200–203, 205–206

painting 192–209
    preparation 194–195, 197–199
    troubleshooting 207–209
199–200
pans 81–83
parsley 95–96
pasta 111
peas 106
pepper 108–109, 113
peppermint oil 33
petroleum jelly 33
pillows 64
pipes 218
planning 8
polish 32 (see also beeswax, wax)
potatoes 38, 83, 98, 109
poultry 120–123
power supply 218, 219

refrigerator 75–76, 85, 98, 99
rice 110–111, 113
rust 18, 65

salt 37, 73, 141
sauces 113–114
screws 220–221
shopping 87–89
shower curtains 66, 67
shower head 67
shower screens 66
silver 60–61
    silver dip 61, 70
skincare 163–174
    cleansing creams 166–167
    hands184, 186–187
    feet 184–186
    moisturising 169-170
    toning 68
smoke alarm 219
soft furnishings 48–51
    removing pet hairs 50
soups 112–113

spices 113–114
sprouts 107
stain removers 138–141
stains 142–149
  beer, 142
  bird droppings 145
  blood 144
  candle wax 144
  chewing gum 143
  coffee 69, 142
  collar grime 145
  curry 143
  fruit juice 143
  egg 79
  grass/mud 146
  ink 147
  make-up 146-147
  perfume 148
  perspiration 148
  scorching 82
  tea 69, 142
  tomato 143
  wine 142
stews 112–113
storage 9, 10
store cupboard 91–98
sugar 126

taps 66, 70
teeth 182–183
tomatoes 98, 108
toothbrush11, 67, 149
toothpaste 29, 57, 58
tumble drier 150

upholstery 48-51
  care label 48–49

vacuum 20
vacuum cleaner 20
vacuum flask 84
vacuuming 7, 16, 19, 27, 30

valuables 8
varnish 53
vases 58
vegetables 92–98, 106–109
  cooking 107
  freezing 102
vinegar 17, 26, 56, 77, 78

wallpaper 40–42, 209–217
  cleaning 40–42, 197
  hanging 215
  pasting 214
  patching 41
  troubleshooting 216–217
walls 40–42
washing machine 134
washing soda 19, 65 (see also
limescale remover)
washing up 78–80
wax polish 54, 55, 56
  removal 56
white spirit 14
windows 43–45
  glass-cleaner 43–44
windowsill cleaner 43
wood 56–58
  scratches 58
  water marks 57
woodwork 42, 220–223

yoghurt 119

BIBLIOGRAPHY

DIY Encyclopedia, Maria Costantino, Parragon, 2002

Herbs: Gardens, Decoctions and Recipes, Emilie Tolley and Chris Mead, Clarkson N Potter Inc, 1985

More for Your Money, Shirley Goode & Erica Griffiths, Penguin 1981

The Food Pharmacy Cookbook, Jean Carper, Simon & Shuster, 1991

Good Housekeeping 'Complete Book of the Home', Ebury Press, 1994

Good Housekeeping, 'Complete Book of Household Hints & Tips', Ebury Press, 1999

Readers Digest 'How to do Just about Anything', Readers Digest, 1988

Household Hints and Handy Tips, Readers Digest, 1992

The Cook's Companion, Susan Campbell, Macmillan,

Home Management, Phyliss Davidson, B.T Batsford,

How to Clean Everything, Alma Chestnut Moore, Tom Stacey,

Supertips to Make Life Easy, Moira Bremner, Coronet Books,

Supertips 2, Moira Bremner, Andre Deustsche

Tips and Wrinkles, Mary Sansbury & Anne Fowler, Pan Books
•

PICTURE CREDITS

Photographs pp 6, 7, 18t, 22, 23, 35b, 36t, 37t, 45, 48, 62t, 63, 65, 69, 70, 71br, 72, 78, 81t, 86, 114t, 117b, 118, 134, 135, 143, 163, 165, 166, 170, 171, 173m, 174, 175b, 182b, 183t, 184, 185m, 185b, 186, 187, 189, 225, 228, 230, 231b, 234, 240, 242, 243, © Getty images

Photographs pp 40, 43, 53, 55, 59, 60b, 74b, 77b, 81b, 85, 87, 88, 93, 96, 103, 105, 106, 107t, 108, 148, 152b, 157, 161, 173t, 173b, 177, 181, 190t, 191, 192, 193t, 194, 197, 203, 218b, 237b, 239b, 244, 245, 246, 248, 249, © Stockbyte

Photographs pp110, 167, 175t, by Paul Forrester

Illustrations pp169, 178, 180, by David Ashby